VALE OF YORK AND YORKSHIRE WOLDS

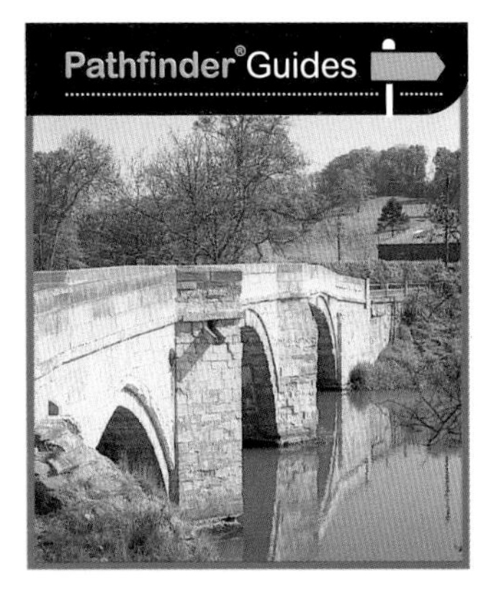

Outstanding Circular Walks

Revised by
Dennis and Jan Kelsall

Acknowledgements
Our thanks to staff of the Yorkshire County Councils, the Tourist Board, other organisations and the many individuals for their help and co-operation in preparing this guide.

Text:	Originally compiled by Brian Conduit. Revised text since the 2009 edition, Dennis and Jan Kelsall
Photography:	Brian Conduit, Dennis and Jan Kelsall Front cover: © John Potter/Alamy Stock Photo
Editorial:	Ark Creative (UK) Ltd
Design:	Ark Creative (UK) Ltd

ISBN: 978-0-31909-073-2

While every care has been taken to ensure the accuracy of the route directions, the publishers cannot accept responsibility for errors or omissions, or for changes in details given. The countryside is not static: hedges and fences can be removed, field boundaries can alter, stiles can be replaced by gates, footpaths can be rerouted and changes in ownership can result in the closure or diversion of some concessionary paths. Also, paths that are easy and pleasant for walking in fine conditions may become slippery, muddy and difficult in wet weather, while stepping stones across rivers and streams may become impassable.

If you find an inaccuracy in either the text or maps, please write to Crimson Publishing at the address below.

First published 2002 by Jarrold Publishing. Revised and reprinted 2005 and 2007.

This edition first published in Great Britain 2009 by Crimson Publishing and reprinted with amendments in 2014, 2017 and 2019.

Crimson Publishing, 19-21D Charles Street, Bath, BA1 1HX

www.pathfinderwalks.co.uk

Printed in India by Replika Press Pvt. Ltd. 7/19

A catalogue record for this book is available from the British Library.

Front cover: Weir on the River Derwent at Kirkham Priory
Previous page: Kirkham Bridge

Contents

Contents

Approximate walk times

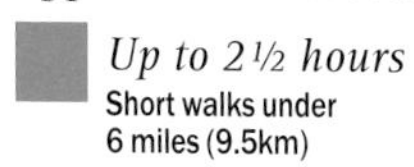
Up to 2½ hours
Short walks under 6 miles (9.5km)

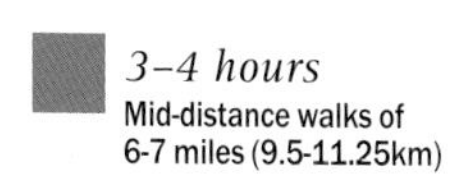
3–4 hours
Mid-distance walks of 6-7 miles (9.5-11.25km)

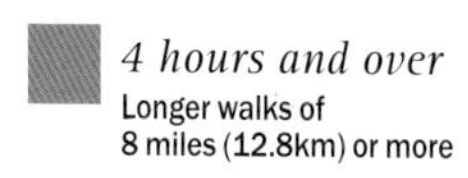
4 hours and over
Longer walks of 8 miles (12.8km) or more

The walk times are provided as a guide only and are calculated using an average walking speed of 2½mph (4km/h), adding one minute for each 10m (33ft) of ascent, and then rounding the result to the nearest half hour.

SCALE 1:250 000 or 1 INCH to 4 MILES *1CM to 2.5KM*

KILOMETRES 0 2 4 6 8 10 15

MILES 0 2 4 6 8 10

KEYMAP HEIGHTS SHOWN IN METRES

Caravans Prohibited

Sinderby, Ainderby Quernhow, Howe, A61, Carlton Miniott, Sowerby, B1448, A170, Osgodby Hall, Bagby, Kilburn, Oldstead, Wass, Byland Abbey, Ampleforth, Abbey College, Skipton-, Sinderby, Great Thirkleby, Carlton Husthwaite, Coxwold, Shandy Hall, Newburgh Priory, Gilling Castle, Dalton, Norton Conyers, A1, Asenby, Raintion, Sessay, Thormanby, Husthwaite, Oulston, A61, A168, Crakehill, Yearsley, Rainton Services, Dishforth, Cundall, Fawdington, Sharow, Dishforth Airfield, RIPON, Copt Hewick, Marton-le-Moor, Norton-le-Clay, Brafferton, Raskelf, Crayke, Bridge Hewick, Helperby, Easingwold, B6265, Littlethorpe, Kirby Hill, Skelton on Ure, Newby Hall, Boroughbridge, ISVRIVM, Tholthorpe, Stillington, Langthorpe, Aldborough, Myton-on-Swale, Alne, Cross Lanes, Huby, Bishop Monkton, Flawith, Roecliffe, Lower Dunsforth, Minskip, DERE STREET, River Ure, Tollerton, Burton Leonard, Grafton, Aldwark, Youlton, A1(M), Upper Dunsforth, South Stainley, Staveley, A6055, Marton, Toll, Linton-on-Ouse, Brearton, Arkendale, Great Ouseburn, Newton-on-Ouse, A19, Farnham, A168, Little Ouseburn, Scotton, Ferrensby, B6265, River Ouse, Thorpe Underwood, Nun Monkton, Shipton, Coneythorpe, Scriven, Beningbrough, B1363, KNARESBOROUGH, Flaxby, Whixley, Green Hammerton, Skelton, Castle, A59, Moor Monkton, Nether Poppleton, HARROGATE, Goldsborough, Kirk Hammerton, Upper Poppleton, Rawcliffe, Great Yorkshire Showground, River Nidd, Cattal, Marston Moor, Walshford, Hunsingore, Little Ribston, Tockwith 1644, Hessay, A59, Knapton, Plumpton Rocks, North Deighton, B6164, Cowthorpe, ROMAN ROAD, Hutton Wandesley, Rufforth, Follifoot, Spofforth, A168, Bickerton, B1224, Castle, Kirk Deighton, A661, A1237, A1036, WETHERBY, B1224, Bilton in Ainsty, Askham Richard, Askham Bryan, Stockeld Park, Kirkby Overblow, Walton, Angram, Sicklinghall, Healaugh, Clap Gate, Linton, Boston Spa, Trading Estate, Wighill, Bilbrough, Copmanthorpe, Collingham, Netherby, Catterton, York Services, Harewood, Thorp Arch, Newton Kyme, Acaster Malbis, Harewood House, A1, A659, A64, Colton, East Keswick, A58, Clifford, TADCASTER, Appleton Roebuck, Bardsey, Eccup Reservoir, Bramham, River Wharfe, Holme Green, River Ouse, Kirby Wharfe, Bolton Percy, Acaster Selby, B1222, Bramham Park, Stutton, Scarcroft, Kiddal Lane End, Ulleskelf, Thorner, Cock Beck, Towton, Ryther, Kelfield, P&R, A6120, Shadwell, A162, Chapel Allerton, A64, Scholes, Aberford, A1(M), B1217, Saxton, Cawood, B6157, Barwick in Elmet, Church Fenton, Roundhay, ROMAN RIDGE, Barkston Ash, Wistow, B1223, Headingley, Pendas Fields, Lotherton Hall, Little Fenton, Biggin, B6159, GARFORTH, B1222, A64, Temple Newsam House, Sherburn in Elmet, Depot, LEEDS, Micklefield, Newthorpe, Thorpe Willoughby, M1, South Milford, A123, A63, Hambleton, B6137, Lumby, Beeston, Swillington, Kippax, Monk Fryston, A63, River Aire, A642, Ledsham, Gateforth, Canal, M621, A639, Great Preston, A1246, Woodlesford, Ledston, A162, Hillam, Selby, A653, Middleton, Robin Hood, M1, Oulton, A656, Fairburn, Burton Salmon, West Haddlesey, Birkin, ROTHWELL, Mickletown, A654, Carlton, Methley, Allerton Bywater, Chapel Haddlesey, New Fryston, East Ardsley, Lofthouse, B6135, CASTLEFORD, Brotherton, Beal

Keymap 1

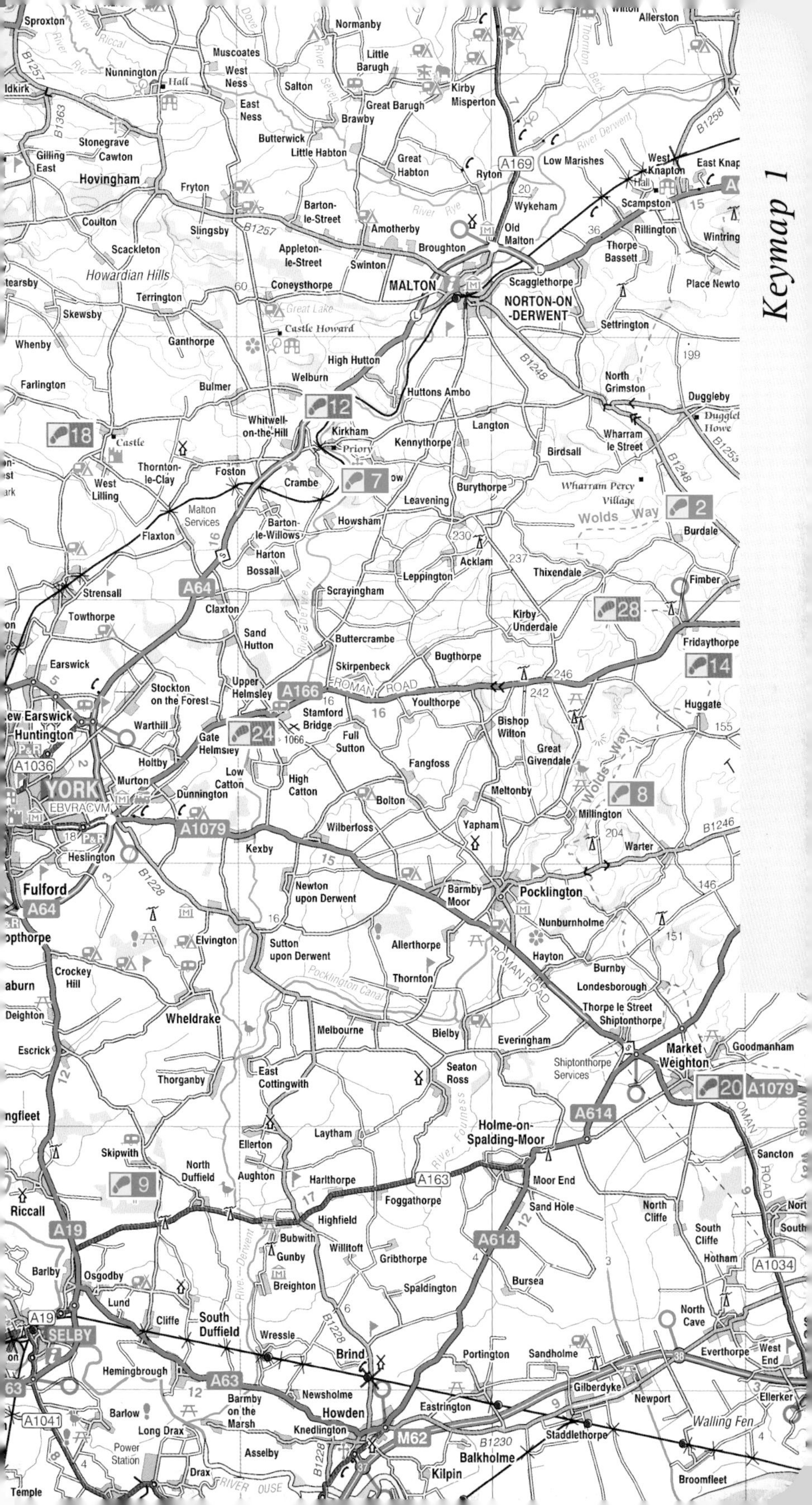

Sproxton
Normanby
Allerston
Muscoates
Little Barugh
Nunnington
Hall
West Ness
Salton
Kirby Misperton
Great Barugh
East Ness
Brawby
Butterwick
Little Habton
Great Habton
Ryton
A169
Low Marishes
West Knapton
East Knapton
Scampston
Stonegrave
Cawton
Gilling East
Hovingham
Fryton
Barton-le-Street
Wykeham
Rillington
Wintringham
Coulton
Slingsby
B1257
Amotherby
Broughton
Old Malton
Thorpe Bassett
Scackleton
Appleton-le-Street
Swinton
Howardian Hills
MALTON
Scagglethorpe
Place Newton
Terrington
Coneysthorpe
NORTON-ON-DERWENT
Skewsby
Great Lake
Castle Howard
Settrington
Whenby
Ganthorpe
High Hutton
Welburn
North Grimston
Farlington
Bulmer
B1248
Duggleby
Huttons Ambo
Whitwell-on-the-Hill
Kirkham
Priory
Langton
Wharram le Street
Castle
Kennythorpe
Birdsall
Thornton-le-Clay
Foston
Crambe
Burythorpe
Wharram Percy Village
West Lilling
Leavening
Wolds Way
Malton Services
Barton-le-Willows
Howsham
Burdale
Flaxton
Harton
Acklam
Bossall
Leppington
Thixendale
Fimber
Strensall
Scrayingham
Claxton
Towthorpe
Kirby Underdale
A64
Sand Hutton
Buttercrambe
Fridaythorpe
Earswick
Bugthorpe
Skirpenbeck
Stockton on the Forest
Upper Helmsley
A166
Roman Road
Youlthorpe
Huggate
New Earswick
Stamford Bridge
Bishop Wilton
Huntington
Warthill
Gate Helmsley
1066
Full Sutton
Great Givendale
P&R
A1036
Holtby
Fangfoss
Low Catton
High Catton
Murton
YORK
EBVRACVM
Dunnington
Bolton
Meltonby
Millington
A1079
Wilberfoss
Yapham
B1246
Heslington
Kexby
Warter
Fulford
Newton upon Derwent
Barmby Moor
Pocklington
A64
B1228
Nunburnholme
Copmanthorpe
Elvington
Sutton upon Derwent
Allerthorpe
Hayton
Crockey Hill
Pocklington Canal
Thornton
Burnby
Naburn
Londesborough
Deighton
Wheldrake
Thorpe le Street
Shiptonthorpe
Melbourne
Bielby
Everingham
Market Weighton
Goodmanham
Escrick
Seaton Ross
Shiptonthorpe Services
East Cottingwith
Thorganby
A614
Stillingfleet
Holme-on-Spalding-Moor
Laytham
Ellerton
River Foulness
Sancton
Skipwith
North Duffield
Aughton
Harlthorpe
A163
Moor End
Foggathorpe
Sand Hole
North Cliffe
Riccall
Highfield
South Cliffe
A19
Bubwith
Willitoft
Gribthorpe
Gunby
Hotham
Barlby
Osgodby
A1034
Breighton
Spaldington
Bursea
Lund
South Duffield
North Cave
Cliffe
Wressle
B1228
SELBY
Brind
Portington
Sandholme
Everthorpe
West End
Hemingbrough
A63
Newsholme
Gilberdyke
Newport
Ellerker
Barmby on the Marsh
Eastrington
Walling Fen
A1041
Barlow
Howden
Staddlethorpe
Long Drax
Knedlington
M62
B1230
Power Station
Asselby
Balkholme
Drax
River Ouse
Kilpin
Broomfleet
Temple Hirst

Keymap 2

SCALE 1:250 000 or 1 INCH to 4 MILES *1CM to 2.5KM*

0 2 4 6 8 10 KILOMETRES 15

0 2 4 6 MILES 8 10

KEYMAP HEIGHTS SHOWN IN METRES

Normanby
Little Barugh
Wilton
Allerston
Brompton
Thornton Beck
THE CARR
Yedingham
Sherburn
East Heslerton
West Heslerton
Wolds Way
East Knapton
A64
Scampston
Rillington
Wintringham
Wykeham
Old Malton
Barton-le-Street
Amotherby
River Rye
B1257
Appleton-le-Street
Swinton
Broughton
Thorpe Bassett
Place Newton
Butterwick
Coneysthorpe
MALTON
Scagglethorpe
NORTON-ON-DERWENT
Great Lake
Castle Howard
Settrington
Helperthorpe
Weaverthorpe
East Lutton
West Lutton
High Hutton
Welburn
B1248
North Grimston
Huttons Ambo
Duggleby
Duggleby Howe
Kirby Grindalythe
12
Whitwell-on-the-Hill
Kirkham Priory
Langton
Kennythorpe
Wharram le Street
B1253
Sledmere
175
21
7
Westow
Birdsall
Crambe
Burythorpe
Wharram Percy Village
2
Leavening
Wolds Way
Barton-le-Willows
Howsham
Burdale
Sledmere House
B1251
B1252
Harton
Bossall
230
Acklam
237
Thixendale
Fimber
155
122
Leppington
Scrayingham
28
River Derwent
Kirby Underdale
A166
Garton-on-the-Wolds
Sand Hutton
Buttercrambe
Fridaythorpe
Wetwang
Elmswell
Skirpenbeck
Bugthorpe
14
B1248
Upper Helmsley
A166
16
ROMAN ROAD
246
242
Youlthorpe
Kelleythorpe
Stamford Bridge
Huggate
Tibthorpe
Kirkburn
24
Full Sutton
Bishop Wilton
155
A614
Great Givendale
Fangfoss
Wolds Way
8
High Catton
Meltonby
North Dalton
Bainton
Bolton
Millington
B1246
Wilberfoss
Yapham
204
Warter
Kexby
Newton upon Derwent
Barmby Moor
Pocklington
146
Middleton-on-the-Wolds
Lund
Nunburnholme
151
16
Sutton upon Derwent
Allerthorpe
Hayton
50
Holme on the Wolds
Lockington
ROMAN ROAD
Kiplingcotes
Burnby
South Dalton
Thornton
Pocklington Canal
Londesborough
Wheldrake
Thorpe le Street
Shiptonthorpe
Etton
Melbourne
Bielby
Everingham
Goodmanham
Market Weighton
20
Cherry Burton
Shiptonthorpe Services
A1079
East Cottingwith
Seaton Ross
River Foulness
ROMAN ROAD
Wolds Way
A614
Holme-on-Spalding-Moor
Laytham
Sancton
144
Bishop Burton
Ellerton
North Duffield
Aughton
Harlthorpe
A163
Moor End
13
Walkington
Foggathorpe
Sand Hole
North Cliffe
South Newbald
Highfield
South Cliffe
B1230
Bubwith
A614
Hotham
A1034
High Hunsley
162
Gunby
Willitoft
Gribthorpe
Breighton
River Derwent
Bursea
Spaldington
South Duffield
B1228
North Cave
South Cave
Wressle
Everthorpe
West End
164
Riplingham
Brind
Portington
Sandholme
A63
Gilberdyke
Newport
Ellerker
Brantingham
Barmby on the Marsh
Newsholme
Howden
Eastrington
Walling Fen
A63
Swanland
Knedlington
M62
B1230
Staddlethorpe
Elloughton
26
Asselby
Balkholme
Kilpin
Broomfleet
Brough
Drax
RIVER OUSE

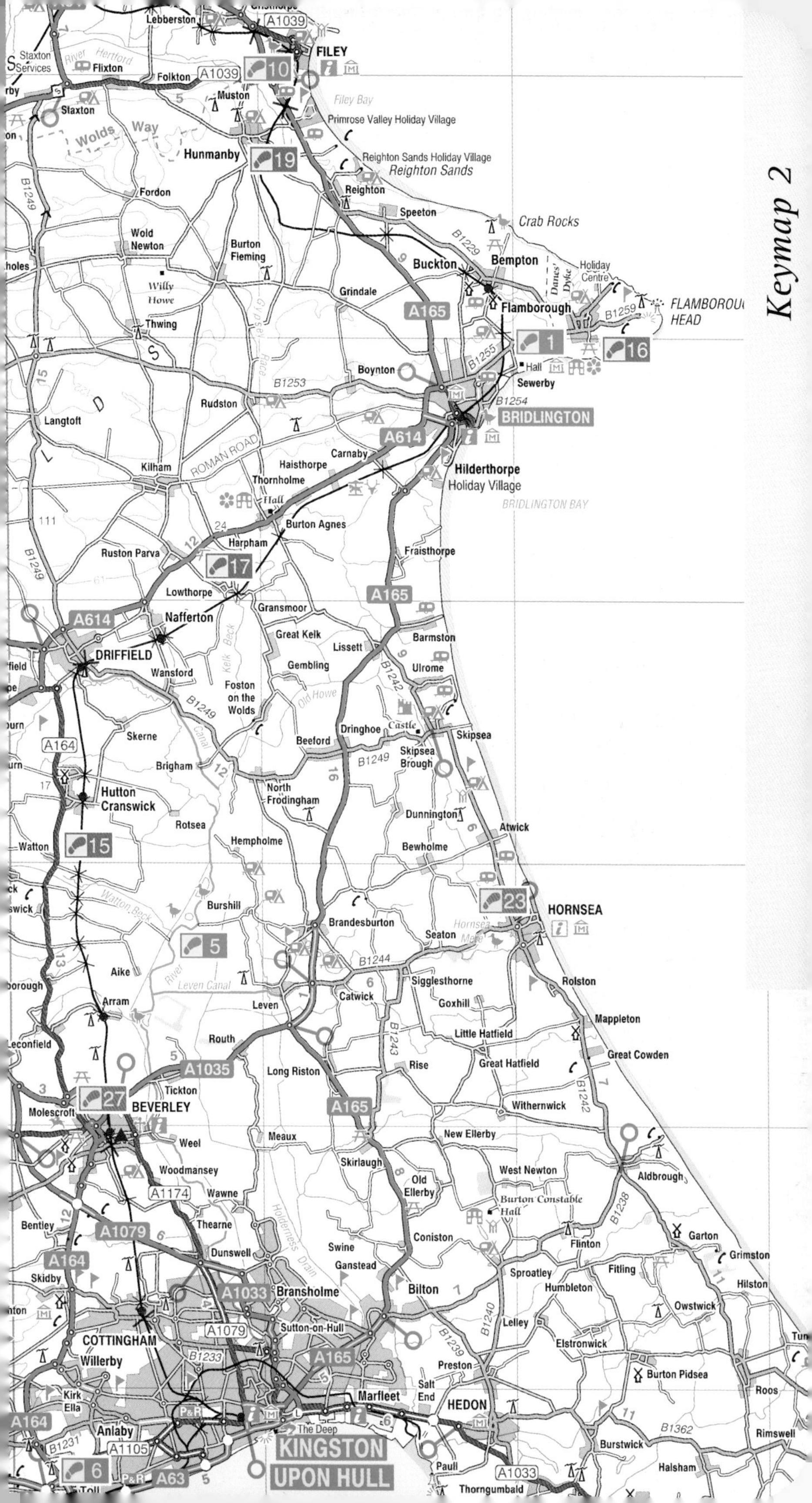

Keymap 2
Lebberston
A1039
FILEY
Staxton Services
River Hertford
Flixton
Folkton
A1039
10
Muston
Filey Bay
Staxton
Primrose Valley Holiday Village
Wolds Way
Hunmanby
19
Reighton Sands Holiday Village
Reighton Sands
Reighton
B1249
Fordon
Speeton
Crab Rocks
Wold Newton
Burton Fleming
B1229
Bempton
Buckton
Danes' Dyke
Holiday Centre
Willy Howe
Grindale
Flamborough
FLAMBOROUGH HEAD
A165
B1259
Thwing
Gypsey Race
1
16
B1255
Boynton
Hall
Sewerby
B1253
B1254
Rudston
Langtoft
BRIDLINGTON
A614
ROMAN ROAD
Carnaby
Kilham
Haisthorpe
Hilderthorpe Holiday Village
Thornholme
Hall
BRIDLINGTON BAY
Burton Agnes
Harpham
B1249
Ruston Parva
17
Fraisthorpe
A165
Lowthorpe
Gransmoor
A614
Nafferton
Barmston
Great Kelk
Lissett
DRIFFIELD
Wansford
Kelk Beck
Gembling
Ulrome
B1242
Foston on the Wolds
Old Howe
B1249
Castle
Skerne
Beeford
Dringhoe
Skipsea
A164
Canal
Skipsea Brough
B1249
Brigham
North Frodingham
Hutton Cranswick
Dunnington
Rotsea
Atwick
Hempholme
Bewholme
Watton
15
23
HORNSEA
Watton Beck
Burshill
Brandesburton
Hornsea Mere
Seaton
5
B1244
River
Aike
Leven Canal
Sigglesthorne
Rolston
Catwick
Arram
Leven
Goxhill
Mappleton
B1243
Little Hatfield
Leconfield
Routh
Great Cowden
A1035
Long Riston
Rise
Great Hatfield
B1242
Tickton
27
A165
BEVERLEY
Withernwick
Molescroft
Weel
Meaux
New Ellerby
Skirlaugh
Woodmansey
West Newton
Old Ellerby
Aldbrough
A1174
Wawne
Burton Constable Hall
B1238
Holderness Drain
Bentley
Thearne
A1079
Coniston
Garton
Swine
Flinton
Grimston
A164
Dunswell
Ganstead
Fitling
Skidby
Sproatley
Bilton
A1033
Bransholme
Humbleton
Hilston
B1240
Owstwick
Lelley
Sutton-on-Hull
A1079
COTTINGHAM
B1239
Elstronwick
Willerby
B1233
A165
Preston
Burton Pidsea
Roos
Kirk Ella
Salt End
Marfleet
HEDON
P&R
A164
The Deep
B1362
Rimswell
Anlaby
Burstwick
KINGSTON UPON HULL
B1231
A1105
Paull
6
P&R
A63
A1033
Halsham
Thorngumbald

Walk	Page	Start	Nat. Grid Reference	Distance	Time	Height Gain
Beverley	85	Beverley, Market Cross	TA 032396	9 miles (14.5km)	4½ hrs	195ft (60m)
Boroughbridge and Aldborough	18	Boroughbridge	SE 396666	4 miles (6.4km)	2 hrs	130ft (40m)
Cowlam and Cottam	64	Cowlam Manor	SE 965654	8 miles (12.9km)	4 hrs	740ft (225m)
Danes' Dyke and Sewerby	14	Danes' Dyke car Park, off B1255	TA 215694	2¾ miles (4.5km)	1½ hrs	180ft (55m)
Flamborough Head	48	Flamborough Head, South Landing	TA 230695	7 miles (11.3km)	3½ hrs	755ft (230m)
Fridaythorpe and Huggate	42	Fridaythorpe	SE 874592	7 miles (11.2km)	3½ hrs	720ft (220m)
Harpham, Burton Agnes and Kilham	51	Bracey Bridge picnic site	TA 076619	7½ miles (12.2km)	3½ hrs	230ft (70m)
Hornsea Mere and the Rail Trail	71	Hornsea, Marine Drive & New Road	TA 208481	8½ miles (13.7km)	4 hrs	N/a
Humber Estuary	24	Humber Bridge Country Park	TA 021259	5½ miles (8.9km)	2½ hrs	N/a
Hunmanby, Muston and Stocking Dale	57	Hunmanby	TA 095774	7½ miles (12.1km)	3½ hrs	490ft (150m)
Kirkham Priory and The River Derwent	26	Kirkham	SE 734658	4¾ miles (7.6km)	2½ hrs	280ft (85m)
Londesborough Park and Goodmanham	60	Market Weighton	SE 877417	7¾ miles (12.5km)	3¾ hrs	410ft (125m)
Millington Dale	28	Millington Wood	SE 837530	4½ miles (7.4km)	2½ hrs	720ft (220m)
Nether Poppleton and the River Ouse	79	Nether Poppleton	SE 564550	9 miles (14.5km)	4 hrs	N/a
Newbald Wold	40	North Newbald	SE 912367	5¾ miles (9.25km)	3 hrs	590ft (180m)
North Cliff and Filey Brigg	32	Filey, The Crescent	TA 118803	5 miles (8km)	2½ hrs	475ft (145m)
Ripon and the rivers Skell and Ure	35	Ripon, Market Place	SE 312712	5½ miles (8.9km)	2½ hrs	165ft (50m)
Sheriff Hutton and Mowthorpe Hill	54	Sheriff Hutton	SE 650663	7½ miles (12.2km)	3½ hrs	525ft (160m)
Skipwith	30	Sandy Lane car park, off Blackwood Road	SE 669377	5½ miles (8.9km)	2½ hrs	N/a
Stamford Bridge	75	Stamford Bridge	SE 711555	8¾ miles (13.9km)	4 hrs	N/a
Tadcaster and Healaugh	68	Tadcaster	SE 487435	8¼ miles (13.3km)	4 hrs	180ft (55m)
Thixendale and Kirby Underdale	89	Thixendale	SE 842611	8¼ miles (13.3km)	4 hrs	935ft (285m)
Tockwith and the River Nidd	20	Tockwith	SE 468523	4¾ miles (7.7km)	2½ hrs	N/a
Tophill Low and Watton Nature Reserves	22	Wilfholme Landing	TA 061471	5 miles (8km)	2½ hrs	N/a
Watton and Kilnwick	45	Watton, the Green	TA 018500	6¾ miles (11km)	3½ hrs	115ft (35m)
Welburn and Castle Howard	38	Welburn	SE 720680	5¾ miles (9.2km)	3 hrs	360ft (110m)
Welton Dale and Brantingham Wold	82	Welton	SE 957272	8¾ miles (14.2km)	4½ hrs	965ft (295m)
Wharram Percy	16	Wharram Percy car park	SE 866644	2¾ miles (4.4km)	1½ hrs	310ft (95m)

Comments

This walk takes you across the pleasant countryside to the south of Beverley. Near the end, there are superb views over the town, minster and the flat lands beyond.

An attractive stretch beside the River Ure is followed by a visit to the site of a Roman town. A brief detour enables you to see three prehistoric monoliths.

An ancient church, an interesting medieval village site and remnants of a Second World War hilltop airfield are brought together in this fine ramble through the Wolds.

There is plenty of interest on this short and straightforward walk: superb coastal views, a wooded ravine, a prehistoric earthwork and an 18th-century hall.

This is a walk of fine seascapes and dramatic cliff scenery as you follow a winding clifftop path around the chalk headland of Flamborough Head.

The walk takes you through a typical Wolds landscape of sweeping uplands and deep, dry valleys, and there are extensive views.

This walk links three attractive villages near the foot of the Wolds and passes a fine Elizabethan mansion.

On the opening stretch you pass by Hornsea Mere, and the return leg makes use of a disused railway track. There are wide views across Holderness.

An invigorating walk beside the Humber Estuary, which is inevitably dominated by the soaring elegance of the Humber Bridge.

The route passes through two attractive villages, and the highlight is a walk along a beautiful wooded dale.

A pleasant walk through woodland and across fields is followed by a beautiful ramble beside the River Derwent. There are fine views of the ruins of Kirkham Priory.

This fine walk in the Wolds includes a market town, two villages, medieval churches, parkland and extensive views across the Vale of York.

Millington is a delightful village, and there are dramatic views over Millington Dale and a lovely optional, but highly recommended, finale through Millington Wood.

A walk across fields to the confluence of the rivers Nidd and Ouse is followed by a lengthy and attractive ramble beside the Ouse.

From the village of North Newbald gentle slopes lead up over the wolds, and there are fine views throughout.

The route includes fine cliff walking, the dramatic headland of Filey Brigg and sweeping views across Filey Bay to Flamborough Head.

There is some delightful riverside walking beside the rivers Skell and Ure in the vicinity of the cathedral city of Ripon.

Starting near the church and castle ruins at Sheriff Hutton, this walk in the Howardian Hills gives you fine views over the Vale of York to the line of the Wolds.

A wander past the site of a wartime aerodrome on one of the last remaining areas of lowland heath in the north of England, an area full of wildlife and interesting plants.

A fine walk along the Derwent valley from Stamford Bridge, the last great Viking battle on British soil and prequel to William of Normandy's invasion in 1066.

The walk takes you across the gently undulating country of the Wharfe valley to the north of Tadcaster.

This is high Wolds country at its finest, with two small but attractive villages, extensive views and a real feeling of remoteness.

There is pleasant walking beside the River Nidd, and the wide views across the Vale of York include the Civil War battlefield of Marston Moor.

Don't forget binoculars for this great walk across the fens bordering the River Hull, which passes two fine bird reserves.

This is a flat walk near the foot of the wolds. Both Watton and Kilnwick have interesting old churches, one of which is on the site of a medieval priory.

Most of the walk is through the grounds of the Castle Howard estate, and there are fine views of the great house and some of the other buildings in the park.

A combination of wooded valleys, open hillsides, grand views and two picturesque villages – both with superb churches – creates a most enjoyable and satisfying walk.

England's most complete deserted medieval village site and its ruined church are the focal points of this fine Wolds walk.

Introduction to the Vale of York and Yorkshire Wolds

Yorkshire is a great area for walking, and it is not surprising that England's largest county contains a wide variety of terrain. For obvious reasons walkers tend to flock to the two national parks, Yorkshire Dales and North York Moors, and to the 'Brontë country' of the South Pennines, but this huge county has much more to offer.

The wide plain of the Vale of York is the very heart of the county, watered by its principal rivers and containing the great city of York. Travelling eastwards across the vale, the western escarpment of the Yorkshire Wolds can be seen on the horizon. These rolling uplands exhibit all the characteristics of chalk country and are the most northerly chalk area in Britain, ending at the dramatic cliffs of Flamborough Head. Unlike other parts of Yorkshire, both the vale and wolds are mainly given over to arable farming, and their gentle landscapes are reminiscent of parts of southern England, a comment one could never make about the sterner terrain of either the Pennines or the North York Moors.

Vale of York

The Vale of York is a large area of predominantly flat country bordered by the Pennines in the west, the Howardian Hills and beyond them the North York Moors in the north-east, and the Yorkshire Wolds in the east. To the south, the vale merges into the flat lands that extend beyond the River Ouse into Lincolnshire and South Yorkshire.

The main rivers through the Vale of York come from the Pennines to the west, flowing down through the Yorkshire Dales and on to the Humber. The Swale, Ure and Nidd join to form the Ouse, which then continues through York. South of the city, the river is enlarged by the Wharfe, Aire and Don and also the Derwent, the latter the only tributary the Ouse receives from the eastern rather than the western moorlands. After the Trent joins the Ouse, beyond Goole, the combined rivers become the mighty Humber Estuary and continue on to the North Sea. Most of these rivers are featured in the selection of walks in this guide, and their embankments provide generally easy and trouble-free walking, as well as giving extensive views across the vale.

At the heart of the vale stands the historic city of York, traditional capital of the North of England. Originally founded by the Romans as Eboracum, it became the capital, both political and ecclesiastical, of the Anglo-Saxon kingdom of Northumbria and, for a time, the centre of a Viking kingdom. Its great minster, seat of the archbishops of York, is the largest medieval church in England and one of the largest in Europe. The city flourished throughout the Middle Ages and later – it was an important inland port – and only when the Industrial Revolution spawned the giant new cities of Leeds, Bradford and Sheffield did York lose its dominant position. However, it still remains, in spirit if not in size, the capital of the North. Apart from the minster, there are a vast number of attractions in the city.

The gatehouse of Kirkham Priory

On the northern edge of the Vale of York, the Howardian Hills – an Area of Outstanding Natural Beauty – act as a sort of buffer between the vale and North York Moors. They offer fine walking, and from their slopes many views encompass both the vale and the wolds.

Yorkshire Wolds

To the east lie the wolds, the northern limits of a continuous band of chalk uplands that extends across the country in a north-easterly direction. From Dorset this band first heads across Salisbury Plain, through the Oxfordshire and Berkshire Downs and on to the Chilterns and the gentle heights of East Anglia. To the north of the Wash, it becomes the Lincolnshire Wolds and finally reappears on the other side of the Humber as the Yorkshire Wolds. The wolds end at Flamborough Head, between Bridlington and Filey.

This is classic chalk country at its finest, a landscape of rolling hills and deep, dry valleys punctuated by small areas of woodland, farms and scattered villages. It is sparsely populated country, and in some of the tiny and remote villages, tucked away in almost secretive valleys, the 21st century

Filey

Kilham

hardly seems to have intruded, which is very much part of their appeal. The large number of place names ending in either -by or -thorpe are an indication of Viking influence in this area and proof of probable large-scale Viking settlement.

York and Beverley are the obvious gateways into the area but the wolds are also ringed by a series of small market towns – Malton, Pocklington, Market Weighton and Driffield – as well as the coastal resorts of Bridlington and Filey.

Compared with the other upland areas of Yorkshire, the wolds are intensively farmed and overwhelmingly arable, although there is some sheep farming. Walking is excellent and, although the slopes are generally gentle, the wolds do rise to more than 800ft (244m) and can provide reasonably challenging routes for the more energetic and adventurous walkers. The walks often follow clear and broad tracks from which there are seemingly endless views across deep valleys and rolling hills. The views from the western escarpment are particularly impressive, looking across the Vale of York.

Holderness

Lying between the wolds, North Sea and Humber Estuary is the roughly triangular-shaped, flat coastal region of Holderness, an area of rich sheep pastures. In the Middle Ages this was a wealthy area, as can be seen from the number of exceptionally large and fine churches that preside over what are now quite small places. Particularly impressive are the churches at Hedon and Patrington, known respectively as the 'king and queen of Holderness'. The finest churches of all are to be found in the delightful and historic town of Beverley, whose skyline is filled not only by the towers of its magnificent minster but also by the almost equally impressive St Mary's Church.

Much of the wealth of these towns came from river trade but in time the many small ports along the Humber and its tributaries – both on the Yorkshire and Lincolnshire banks of the river – were eclipsed by Edward I's new town of Kingston (King's Town), built at the confluence of the Humber and Hull. Here is to be found the largest parish church in the whole of England, and over the centuries Hull developed into one of the world's greatest fishing ports.

The flat coast of Holderness has a number of sandy beaches, and in Victorian times rail links with Hull and the other large cities of Yorkshire led to the development of small seaside resorts at Withernsea and Hornsea. The major resorts were farther north, at Bridlington and Filey, both of which lie on wide sandy bays with superb cliffs.

Although there are no hills in Holderness, the combination of huge skies and open expanses – reminiscent of the Cambridgeshire Fens in some ways – has its attractions so some walks have been included in this relatively little-known area.

Walking in the area

The Wolds Way is the major long-distance route. Starting on the Humber Estuary, within sight of the great bridge, it heads across the wolds to finish at Filey Brigg. Its northern end coincides with the southern end of the Cleveland Way, and the two paths together provide continuously fine walking across a large slice of Yorkshire, from the Humber to Helmsley.

Other long-distance routes include the Minster Way – between York and Beverley – and the Centenary Way. Some disused railway lines have been converted into footpaths and cycleways. These include the Hudson Way, between Beverley and Market Weighton, and the Hornsea Trail, between Hull and Hornsea.

One advantage of walking on this eastern side of England is that it has a drier climate, although the wolds in particular can get heavy snowfalls in winter. Calm days at any time of year can result in the notorious sea-frets (mists) on the North Sea coast but on such days a few miles' journey inland may reward you with sunshine, blue skies and clear conditions.

First-time visitors to this area may well be agreeably surprised by its variety of terrain and excellent walking facilities, whether it be flat and easy strolls beside the rivers of the Vale of York, the dramatic coastal walks near Flamborough Head or the more energetic rambles over the open hillsides and through the steep-sided dales of the chalk wolds.

Danes' Dyke and Sewerby

		GPS waypoints
Start	Danes' Dyke car park, off B1255 between Bridlington and Flamborough	TA 215 694
Distance	2¾ miles (4.5km)	Ⓐ TA 213 693 Ⓑ TA 199 687
Height gain	180 feet (55m)	Ⓒ TA 215 691
Approximate time	1½ hours	
Parking	Danes Dyke	
Ordnance Survey maps	Landranger 101 (Scarborough), Explorers 295 (Bridlington, Driffield & Hornsea) or 301 (Scarborough, Bridlington & Flamborough Head)	

This short but interesting route begins with a descent into a dramatic wooded ravine. After passing an 18th-century country house with fine gardens, the walk returns along the cliff path from where there are extensive views to the nearby resort of Bridlington, with its superb sandy beaches, and the chalk cliffs of Flamborough Head.

Danes' Dyke, above the eastern side of the ravine, is a linear earthwork, about 2½ miles (4km) long, which stretches across the neck of the Flamborough peninsula. Despite its name, it is thought to have been constructed during the Iron Age rather than by the Vikings.

Flamborough Head from Sewerby

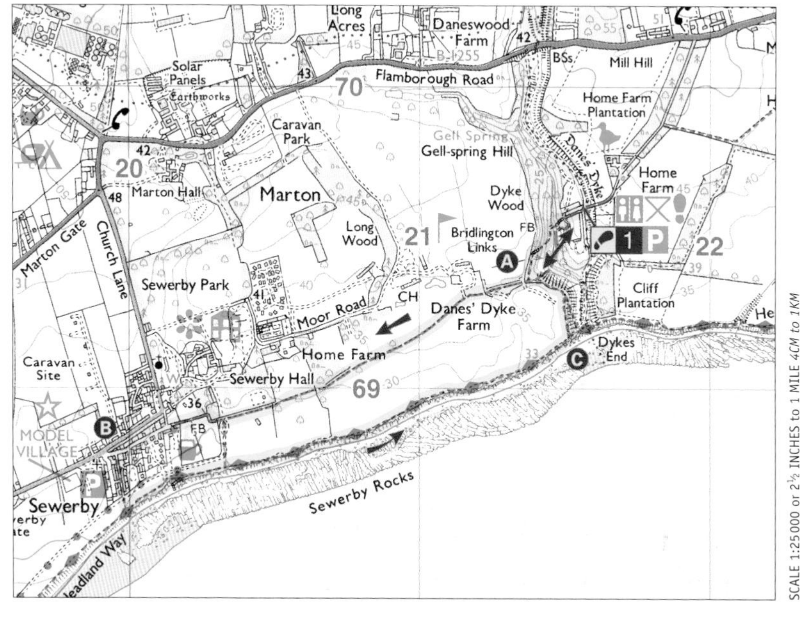

From the car park by the **café** and toilets, walk back along the entrance drive to a junction near the pay machine and go left on a bridleway signed the Headland Way. It drops beside a wall and then steeply down steps into Dyke Wood, crossing a bridge over the stream at the bottom. Swing left to a fork and there bear right, very soon reaching another junction **A**.

Go right and, ignoring crossing golfers' paths, soon pass the ruins of Danes' Dyke Farm on your right. The path continues along a strip of rough dividing the golf course, shortly passing the clubhouse, which lies over to the right. Keep going into a wood, emerging at the far side to cross a meadow. Carry on past the edge of the village cricket green in front of Sewerby Hall, crossing a tarmac path, which leads into the grounds.

Built around 1720, its various rooms reflect the differing styles of the Georgian, Regency and Victorian eras. The park and walled gardens extend over 50 acres (20 hectares) and children will particularly enjoy the zoo.

Maintain your forward direction along a path signed to the village, which winds between animal enclosures of Sewerby Hall's zoo. It finishes in the village by **The Ship Inn.** Walk ahead and continue beyond the pub and **Old Forge Tea Rooms**, almost to the street's end. Just before it merges with the main road, leave along a narrow path on the left **B**.

It runs between the backs of gardens to emerge onto the cliff top promenade. Go left beside a tarmac drive and where it subsequently curves away to the left, keep ahead along the Headland Way towards Danes' Dyke. Go past the cricket green and carry on above Sewerby Rocks. Approaching Danes' Dyke, the path curves from the sea **C**.

Reaching a junction of paths, take the left branch signed to Sewerby Hall, which runs along the rim of the wooded ravine to another junction **A**. Keep ahead and retrace your steps to the car park.

Wharram Percy

Start	Wharram Percy car park, signposted from B1248 between Wharram le Street and Wetwang
Distance	2¾ miles (4.4km)
Height gain	310 feet (95m)
Approximate time	1½ hours
Parking	Wharram Percy
Ordnance Survey maps	Landranger 100 (Malton & Pickering), Explorer 300 (Howardian Hills & Malton)

GPS waypoints

- SE 866 644
- Ⓐ SE 868 634
- Ⓑ SE 858 631
- Ⓒ SE 861 645

Excavation and research spanning more than 50 years has made Wharram Percy the most famous of Britain's 3,000 or so deserted medieval villages. It is the focal point of this short but spectacular walk, which encircles the dale to approach from the south from where the best view is to be had.

Turn right from the car park along the lane and follow it for ½ mile (800m) to a sharp right-hand bend. Where the lane subsequently curves left, keep ahead through a gate Ⓐ along a track signed as the Centenary Way. Beyond a wood, walk on along the top of an expansive field to exit through a gate at its far end Ⓑ.

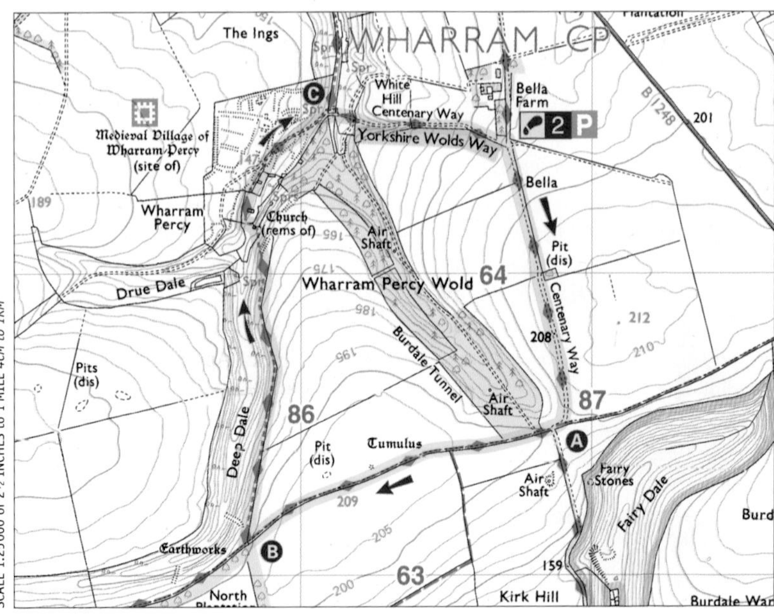

Joining the Yorkshire Wolds Way, swing right towards Wharram Percy on a path that runs above Deep Dale, affording an impressive view into the valley. After a while, turning a slight bend, the ruined church of the abandoned settlement comes spectacularly into sight. Just beyond that point, look for a waymark that directs the path on an angle down the slope, heading directly towards the church.

Through a kissing-gate at the bottom, carry on around a small pond to another gate into the churchyard. Leaving at the far side, walk past the site of the old vicarage to yet another gate beside a couple of mid-19th century cottages.

Archaeological evidence shows settlement in the valley since Neolithic times, but it is during the medieval period that it peaked as a prosperous farming community. Mounds and hollows indicate the extent of the village cottages and gardens, while larger fields extended onto the wold. At the centre stood the church, the only building to survive after the last villagers were evicted early in the 16th century to make way for more profitable sheep walks. Until the church at Thixendale was opened in 1870, it continued to serve the surrounding dales, but then gradually fell out of use and finally closed in 1949.

Beyond the cottages, the path rises between foundations of the 18th-century farmstead to meet another path. Go right past grassy mounds, all that remains of the medieval cottages. At the bottom, leave through a gate and cross a track to a footbridge over a brook Ⓒ.

Climb to the pasture above and bear right to another gate on the opposite side. Still following Yorkshire Wolds Way signs, the ongoing path ascends along the base of a narrow fold to return you to the car park. ●

Wharram Percy

Boroughbridge and Aldborough

Start	Boroughbridge
Distance	4 miles (6.4km)
Height gain	130 feet (40m)
Approximate time	2 hours
Parking	Boroughbridge
Ordnance Survey maps	Landranger 99 (Northallerton & Ripon),Explorer 299 (Ripon & Boroughbridge)

GPS waypoints

- Start: SE 396 666
- A: SE 391 664
- B: SE 399 666
- C: SE 398 670
- D: SE 411 667
- E: SE 405 661

After a short detour to an impressive group of standing stones dating from 2,700BC, this pleasant walk takes a roundabout route beside the River Ure to nearby Aldborough, whose Roman past is revealed in a small museum.

The pleasant town of Boroughbridge grew around a Norman river crossing, just upstream of the Roman town. The bridge itself has been rebuilt many times during the centuries, the most notable instance following collapse in 1945, when a transporter carrying an 85-ton load optimistically attempted to cross.

(Start) The walk begins from the ornate fountain in St James' Square. To see the Devil's Arrows, cross to **The Black Bull** and walk along St Helena, branching left to the main road. Go left and then almost immediately right along Roecliffe Lane. You will find the 'arrows' a little less than 1/4 mile (400m) along, two in the right-hand field and the other to the left of the lane **A**.

It is thought there were originally five pillars, one lost in time and another broken during the 16th century to provide stone for a bridge across the River Tutt. A plausible theory suggests an alignment with midsummer moonrise, but their true purpose will never be known. They are none the less impressive; the largest standing over 22 feet (6.7m) high and taller than any other in the country apart from Stonehenge.

Return to St James' Square and continue past **The Malt Shovel** along Aldborough Road. Where it shortly bends, take the minor road towards Aldborough, walking for another 150 yds to a footpath signed through a kissing-gate on the left **B**. It leads across the fields to the River Ure.

Climbing onto the embankment **C**, follow the meandering riverside path downstream for a little over 1 1/4 miles (2km) until you eventually drop out onto a track **D**.

Follow it right to meet a lane and go right again towards Aldborough. Approaching the village, branch off left and then keep left to pass the central open green. Continue up to the top of the street, following it around right to

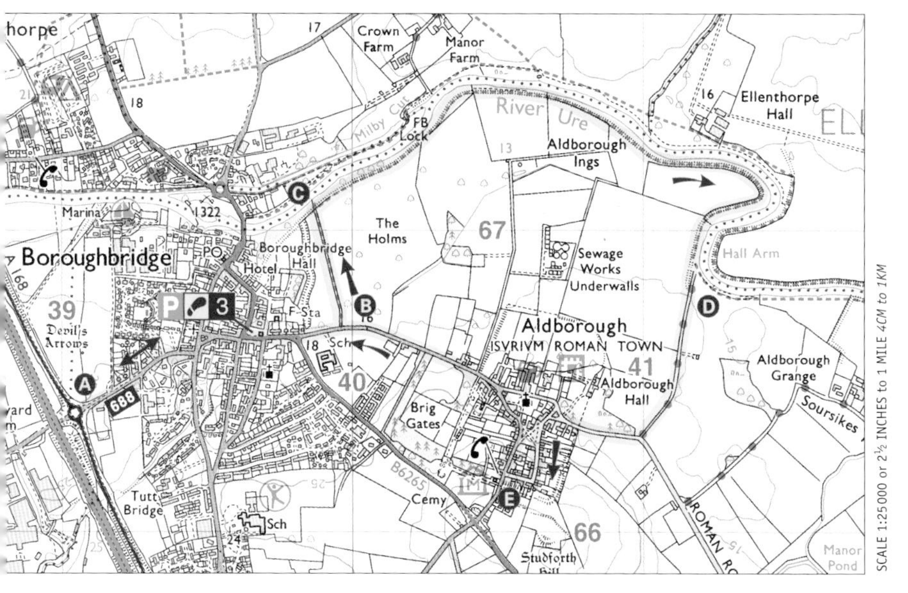

0 200 400 600 800 METRES 1 KILOMETRES
0 200 400 600 YARDS ½ MILES

a junction. The entrance to the Roman town and museum is then just to the left **E**.

The Romans established Isurium Brigantium in AD71, guarding the point at which Dere Street from York crossed the river. A civil settlement later developed around the military encampment and after the Romans left Britain, it continued as the principal town of the Romanised Brigantes. Fragments of the walls remain, but the finest treasures are two splendid mosaic pavements.

Leaving the museum, follow the street down into the village past the other side of the green where stands a tall maypole. Now keep left past the church to meet the main lane. **The Ship Inn** lies just to the right – otherwise turn left for your return to Boroughbridge.

The River Ure near Boroughbridge

Tockwith and the River Nidd

Start	Tockwith
Distance	4¾ miles (7.7km)
Height gain	Negligible
Approximate time	2½ hours
Parking	Roadside parking at Tockwith
Ordnance Survey maps	Landranger 105 (York & Selby), Explorer 289 (Leeds)

GPS waypoints

- SE 468 523
- Ⓐ SE 464 526
- Ⓑ SE 463 535
- Ⓒ SE 463 540
- Ⓓ SE 469 544
- Ⓔ SE 474 535

Much of this walk is along the tracks and field paths between the village of Tockwith and the meandering River Nidd, with a splendid middle section beside the river itself. There are wide views across the Vale of York and, towards the end, the route passes close to the site of the Civil War battlefield of Marston Moor.

The walk begins from the road junction in the centre of the village. Head along Westfield Road in the direction of Cattal and Cowthorpe, passing **The Spotted Ox** and the small Victorian church. Swinging past a junction, the way becomes Fleet Lane, soon reaching a bend where Ness Lane, a track signed as a bridleway, leaves on the right Ⓐ.

After 350 yds, turn off left onto a second track. Just before reaching a barn at its end, leave along a hedged grass track on the right Ⓑ. Through a kissing-gate where it finishes, walk along a pasture to another gate in the far-right corner and keep straight ahead on a path crossing the crop of the subsequent field. Negotiate a final kissing-gate to climb onto the flood embankment bordering the River Nidd Ⓒ.

As you follow the river downstream around a sweeping horseshoe bend, there are views across the Vale of York where the

The River Nidd near Tockwith

Saxon church at Kirk Hammerton can be glimpsed in the distance. Negotiating periodic stiles, the path eventually passes a substantial old mill on the opposite bank, shortly after which is a double stile (the second encountered along the way) **D**.

Over the first stile, turn right and walk away along a fenced path. It finishes over a bridge to meet a gravel track. Go left and, eventually reaching a T-junction, turn right along a tarmac track. Before long, however, leave it through a gate on the left and follow a grass track atop an embankment, Moor Lane.

Through a gate where it finishes **E**, go right along another track, Kendal Lane. The low-lying fields stretching away to the left are the site of the biggest battle of the Civil War, Marston Moor. In July 1644, Prince Rupert's army suffered a crushing defeat at the hands of Cromwell's well-disciplined troops, a setback from which Charles I never recovered his position. There is a memorial beside the lane a mile (1.6km) to the east of Tockwith. Reaching the end of the track, follow the lane right back into the centre of the village. ●

0 200 400 600 800 METRES 1 KILOMETRES
0 200 400 600 YARDS ½ MILES

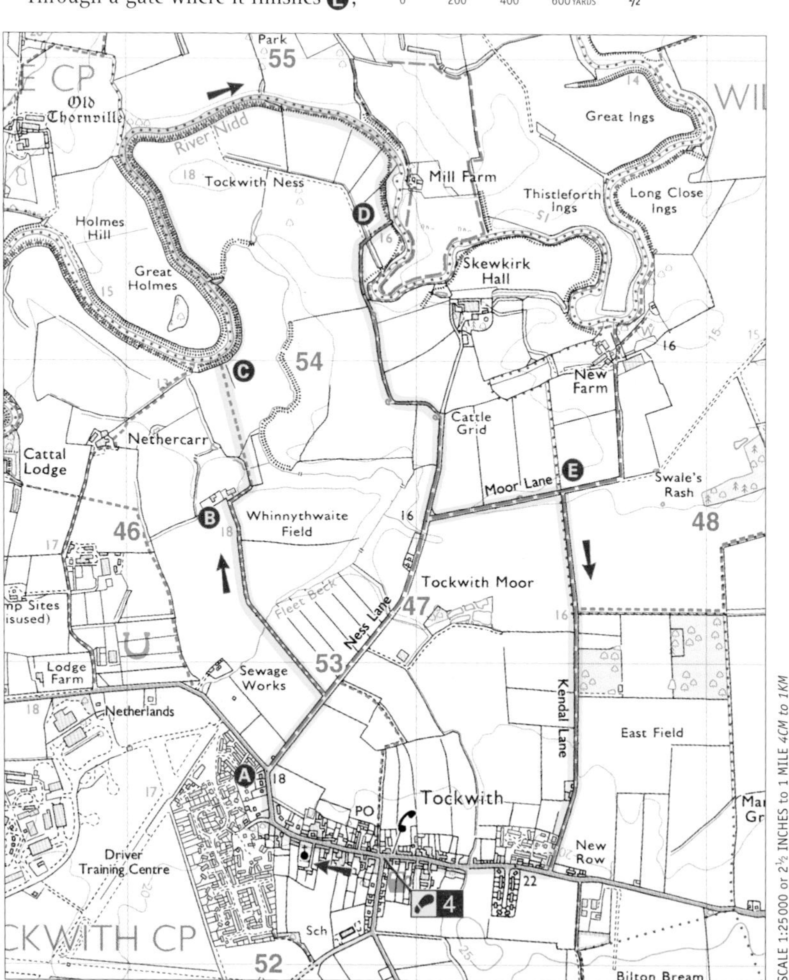

SCALE 1:25 000 or 2½ INCHES to 1 MILE *4CM to 1KM*

Tophill Low and Watton Nature Reserves

Start	Wilfholme Landing – 3 miles (5km) south-east of Watton, off A164
Distance	5 miles (8km)
Height gain	Negligible
Approximate time	2½ hours
Parking	Wilfholme Landing
Ordnance Survey maps	Landranger 106 (Market Weighton), Explorer 295 (Bridlington, Driffield & Hornsea)

GPS waypoints

- Start TA 061 471
- A TA 064 474
- B TA 069 483
- C TA 078 499
- D TA 072 500
- E TA 062 495
- F TA 064 485

Bird watchers will delight in this meandering stroll beside the ditches draining Watton Carrs. Open fields, woods, marshland, pools, and the River Hull between them attract a huge diversity of birdlife, showcased in two reserves. Access to Tophill Low Reserve requires a permit, obtainable from the Visitor Centre car park.

From a gate behind the parking area, a bridleway is signed onto the embankment beside the River Hull. Almost immediately forced left by the outflow of Watton Beck, through gates turn over a bridge and go right again to resume your northerly course by the river. Shortly reaching the boundary of the Tophill Low Nature Reserve A, the waymarked path drops beside the Beverley and Barmston Drain.

The way runs pleasantly through a grove of trees, where a break reveals the neighbouring Watton Reserve, encountered at closer quarters later on. Walk for ½ mile (800m) to a bridge crossing the drain at the entrance to Tophill Low Waterworks and Nature Reserve B.

To reach the Visitor Centre, follow the drive right around the perimeter to the north-eastern corner of the plant. There are several hides overlooking the various lagoons and reservoirs of the reserve, where there is generally much to see throughout the year.

The walk, however, continues beside the drain for another mile (1.6km) and, although little is visible of the reserve, there is a grand view to the west across low-lying fields and marsh broken by clumps of woodland.

Reaching a narrow footbridge C, cross and walk away at the field edge. Continue through a gate in the next field, passing Standingholme Farm over to the left. Crossing a stile out of the corner by a wood, immediately go left over a second stile and walk within the fringe of the trees to emerge onto a tarmac farm track D.

Go right, eventually passing another farm, Decoy House. Carry on for a further 300 yds to find a waymark defining a path off left beside Decoy Drain E. It runs at the edge of a couple of large fields before meeting another narrow lane opposite Easingwold Farm F.

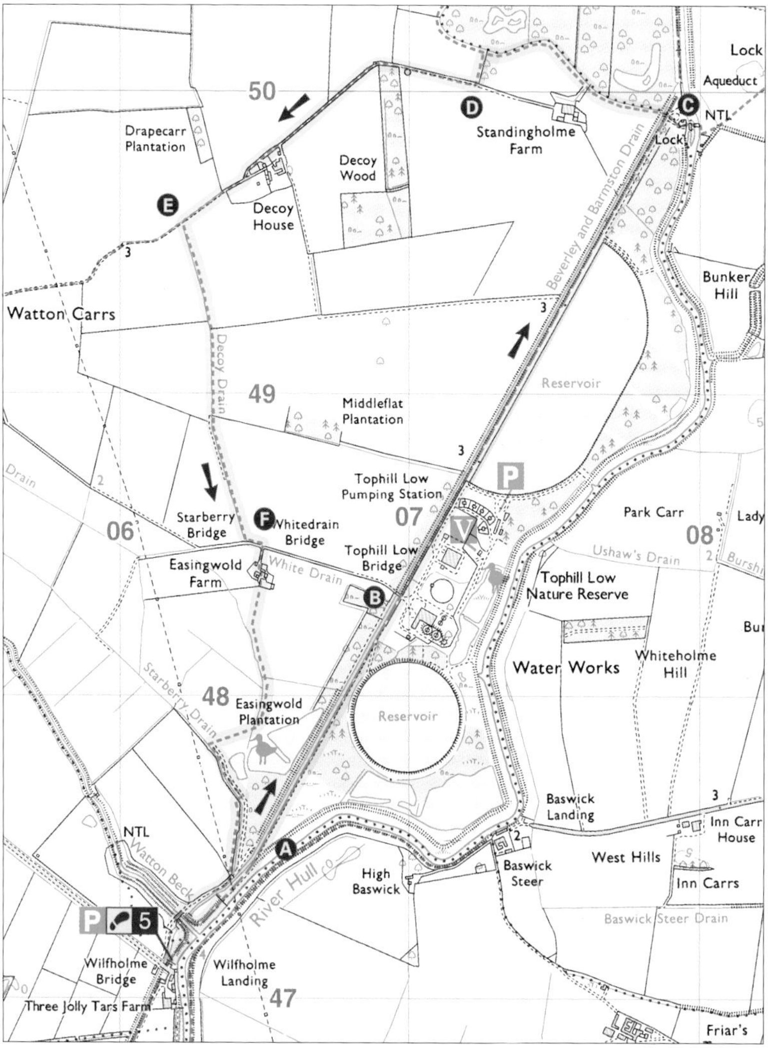

Cross to the entrance track, but where that then bends left into the yard, keep ahead past a brick shippon to a gate. Bear left to a wide opening and head away at the edge of rough grazing with a fence on your left. Keep going beyond its end with a shallow ditch now on your right, which quickly disappears within a hedge. Over a stile hidden in the corner, a narrow path to the right winds on through thicket. Breaking into more open ground, keep going to meet Starberry Drain. Turn left, soon passing a hide, which overlooks the reedy lagoon of the Watton Reserve. After crossing the drain, leave the reserve over a stile. Back beside the Beverley and Barmston Drain, pass through a couple of gates and climb onto the embankment to retrace your outward steps to the parking area.

Humber Estuary

Start	Humber Bridge Country Park
Distance	5½ miles (8.9km)
Height gain	Negligible
Approximate time	2½ hours
Parking	Humber Bridge Country Park
Ordnance Survey maps	Landranger 106 (Market Weighton), Explorer 293 (Kingston upon Hull & Beverley)

GPS waypoints

Start	TA 021 259
A	TA 022 253
B	SE 989 252
C	SE 986 251

This is a 'there and back' walk along the north shore of the Humber Estuary from the Humber Bridge to North Ferriby. The going is easy but be prepared for invigorating breezes sweeping across the river. The views across the estuary towards Lincolnshire are dominated by the soaring elegance of the bridge during the return.

The Humber Bridge, a marvel of 20th-century engineering is one of the longest single-span suspension bridges in the world and a most impressive structure. The length of the main span is 4,626ft (1,410m). It took nine years to build and was opened in 1981. The Country Park, comprising around 50 acres (20 ha) of attractive woodland and meadows, was created from a disused chalk quarry.

From the Tourist Information Centre, walk down the car park to leave at the bottom right corner. Signed to the Humber Bridge Country Park, the path crosses a cycleway to intercept a tarmac track. Briefly follow it left and then bear off right towards the Country Park and Hessle Foreshore. Entering trees,

0 200 400 600 800 METRES 1 KILOMETRES
0 200 400 600 YARDS ½ MILES

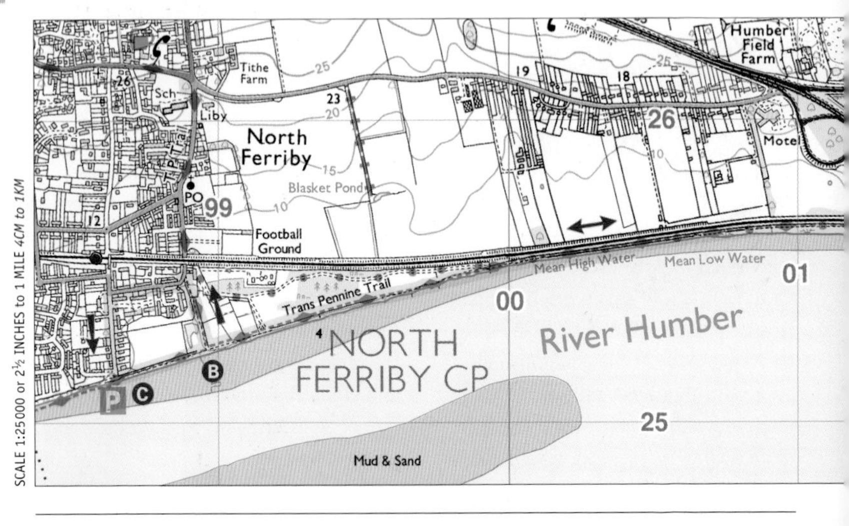

The Humber Bridge

look for a kissing-gate on the right from which a stepped path drops into the now wooded former quarry. Keep ahead past another junction, walking first beneath a railway and then a road bridge. Emerge past the black, brick tower of Cliff Mill onto the foreshore drive beneath the Humber Bridge Ⓐ.

Follow it right to a bend and, if the tide is out, drop beside a Yorkshire Wolds Way sign to continue along the stony beach below the **Country Park Inn** and car park. Not far beyond, look for a waymark directing you back onto

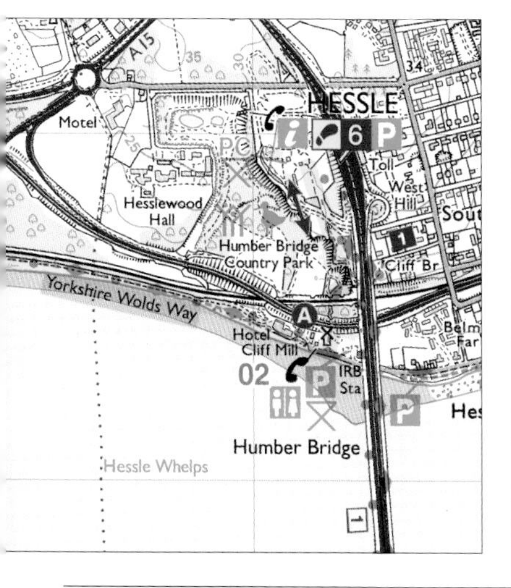

the embankment, along which a track runs to the left through a gate. *If the water is high, remain with the drive past the pub into the car park. Leave at the far end along the embankment track.*

Continue along the embankment, remaining above the riverbank where a divergent path later breaks away. Approaching North Ferriby, keep ahead at a junction, near which three Bronze Age ferryboats were discovered in the mud. A little farther on, just beyond a kissing-gate the ongoing path drops back to the foreshore but is impassable at high tide. However, the path to the right Ⓑ, marked as the High Tide Route, leads past a reedy pond dug in the 19th century to provide clay for a local brick and tile industry. Now flooded with brackish water it is a haven for wildlife.

The path finishes at the corner of a street. Go left and, at the end, go left again to return to the river at a small car park.

Steps over the flood embankment in the left corner Ⓒ lead down to the beach. At low water you can follow the foreshore back to point Ⓑ and retrace your steps to the start. ●

Kirkham Priory and the River Derwent

Start	Kirkham, parking area in front of priory
Distance	4¾ miles (7.6km)
Height gain	280 feet (85m)
Approximate time	2½ hours
Parking	Kirkham Priory (fee – refundable for visitors to Priory)
Ordnance Survey maps	Landranger 100 (Malton & Pickering), Explorer 300 (Howardian Hills & Malton)

GPS waypoints

- Start: SE 734 658
- A: SE 733 657
- B: SE 732 654
- C: SE 738 645
- D: SE 732 635
- E: SE 735 633

The walk begins through woodland before falling across the fields and lanes on the west side of the Derwent Valley. Returning to the river, the route meanders back within the fringe of trees and scrub that borders the bank. The high ground gives fine views across the Vale of York to the wolds and Howardian Hills and towards the end, the ruins of Kirkham Priory make a fine picture on the opposite bank of the Derwent.

The extensive ruins of Kirkham Priory stand in a lovely position above the River Derwent. It was founded as a priory for Augustinian canons in 1125 by Walter l'Espec, who held Helmsley Castle to the north. Legend has it that he endowed the land in memory of his only son, whose untimely death followed a riding accident here. Parts of the church and monastic buildings remain but the most impressive feature of the ruin is the ornate, late 13th-century gatehouse, which bears the heraldic arms of Espec and the de Roos, who succeeded Walter at Helmsley. The community flourished until it was suppressed by Henry VIII in 1539.

Kirkham Bridge and the River Derwent

Start: Follow the lane over the bridge and level crossing, leaving just beyond, as the lane begins to climb, through a gate on the left A. A steep path attacks the wooded valley side, emerging at

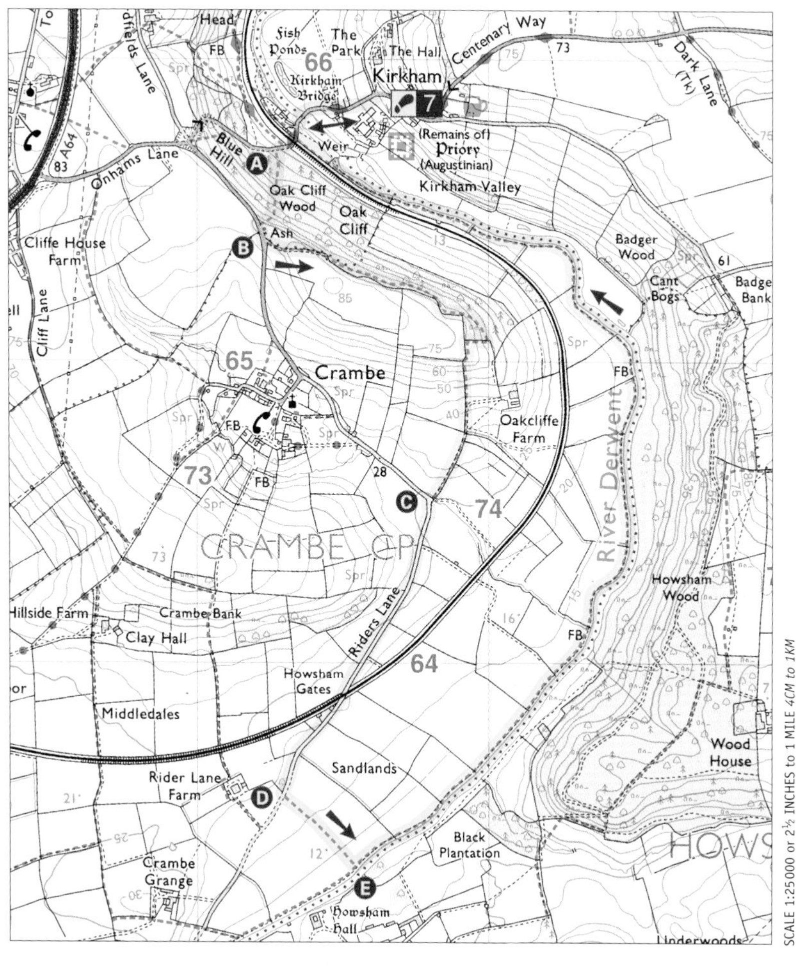

0 200 400 600 800 METRES 1 KILOMETRES
0 200 400 600 YARDS ½ MILES

the top onto the edge of a meadow. Go right to reach a lane and follow it left. After only a few yards turn off onto a gated grass track on the left **B**.

The track leads back to the wood, entering beside a redundant stile. The ongoing path runs within the upper fringe of the trees high above the river for nearly ½ mile (800m) before emerging through a gate onto open pasture. Go right along the field edge and then left within the corner, continuing straight down the hill following an old boundary line to join a track at the bottom coming from Oakcliffe Farm. It leads out to Riders Lane **C**.

Go left, later recrossing the railway line at Howsham Gates. Carry on for a further ¼ mile (400m) to find a path signed off across the field on the left **D**. Through a gate at the far side, continue across grazing and then a rough pasture to a final gate onto the wooded riverbank **E**.

To the left, the return path accompanies the Derwent all the way back to Kirkham Bridge, passing variously through woodland, scrub and at the edge of fields and riverside grazing. Spring and early summer are the best times to see wild flowers and, at any time of the year, you may spot a kingfisher.

Millington Dale

Start	Millington Wood, on minor road between Millington and Huggate
Distance	4½ miles (7.4km). Shorter version 3 miles (4.9km)
Height gain	720 feet (220m). Shorter version 445 feet (135m)
Approximate time	2½ hours. Shorter version 1½ hours
Parking	Millington Wood
Ordnance Survey maps	Landranger 106 (Market Weighton), Explorer 294 (Market Weighton & Yorkshire Wolds Central)

GPS waypoints

Start	SE 837 530
A	SE 829 518
B	SE 839 518
C	SE 844 529
D	SE 841 530
E	SE 836 533
F	SE 832 538

After following the lane along Millington Dale into the village, the route swings back above the opposite flank from where there are grand views across the valley. The full walk includes a pleasant stroll into Millington Wood, a remnant of the ancient woodland that once cloaked the wolds.

(Start) Turning right from the car park, follow the lane up the bank and on to Millington. Keep over the crossroads, but turn left at the next junction by the church (A).

Reaching the bottom, the **The Ramblers' Rest** tearoom lies to the right, however, the onward route is to the left. Just beyond a bend, leave along a track to the right signed as the Minster Way. Where it immediately forks, keep right, dropping through gates to pass Mill Cottage. Ahead, duck boarding leads to a stile, from which the ongoing path climbs straight up the bank to a stile and gate at the top of the field. Ignore it and instead go right beside the fence above the dale to a corner. Cross the stile in front and head uphill, continuing to a stile in the hedge bounding the top of the hill (B).

Turn left past Warren Farm to meet its access, crossing to a track opposite, signed Yorkshire Wolds Way. Carry on along the top edge of the field, from

Millington Dale

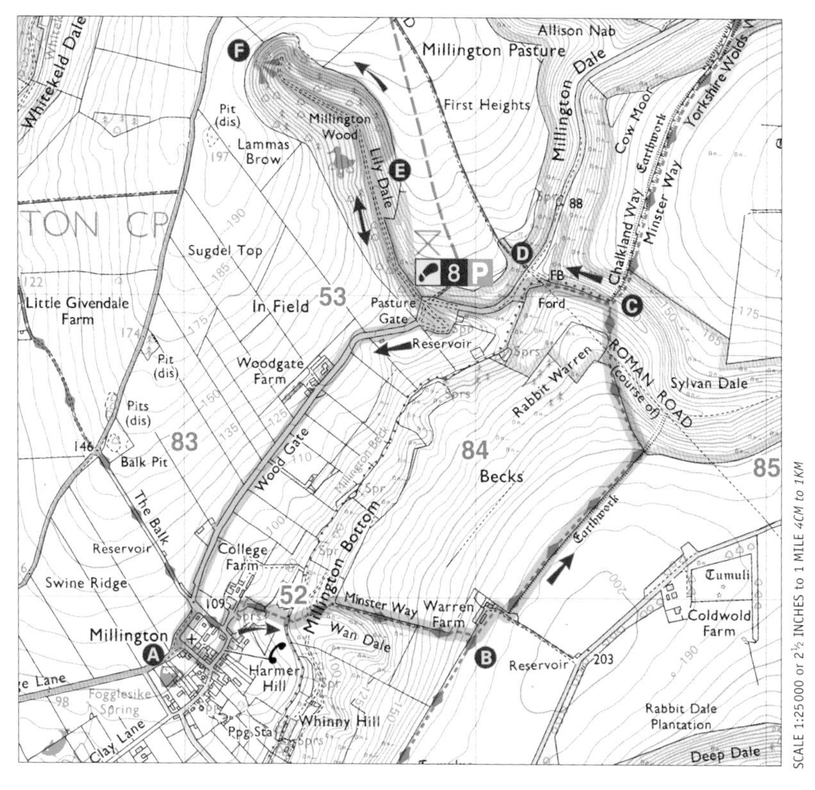

SCALE 1:25 000 or 2½ INCHES to 1 MILE *4CM to 1KM*

0 200 400 600 800 METRES 1 KILOMETRES
0 200 400 600 YARDS ½ MILES

which there is a fine view across to Millington Wood. Swinging within the far corner, head back downhill, leaving at the field bottom through a kissing-gate into Millington Pastures. Strike a slanting course into the dale, going left at a three-way signpost Ⓒ to follow a fence along the base of the valley. Approaching a ford, a path over a stile on the right leads to a footbridge over Millington Beck. Continue up to the lane Ⓓ and go left back to the car park.

There is an equally pleasant 'there and back' walk into Millington Woods, with easy and strenuous options to suit everyone. From a gate at the rear of the car park, a path leads along the valley floor, shortly reaching a partial clearing Ⓔ. The undemanding route simply continues ahead, while the alternative takes the stepped path to the right. Zigzagging up the hillside, it climbs steeply into the trees before settling on a high-level course along the valley side. Eventually meeting another stepped path, go upwards once more, curving around to a 'view point' at the head of the dale Ⓕ. Unfortunately, you cannot see the wood for the trees, but as the ascent deters many people it makes a great spot in which to enjoy a quiet picnic.

For the return, follow the steps all the way to the bottom and walk out along the easy path back to the car park. Charcoal burning has been a traditional occupation here for centuries and the practice is continued as a means of managing this ancient woodland. You'll pass the kiln at some point on the return – its position dependent upon which bit of the wood is being cut.

Skipwith

Start	Sandy Lane car park off Black wood Road, ¾ mile (1.2km) south-east of Skipwith
Distance	5½ miles (8.9km)
Height gain	Negligible
Approximate time	2½ hours
Parking	Car park at start
Ordnance Survey maps	Landrangers 105 (York & Selby) or 106 (Market Weighton, Goole & Stamford Bridge), Explorer 290 (York)

GPS waypoints

- SE 669 377
- Ⓐ SE 659 377
- Ⓑ SE 652 373
- Ⓒ SE 644 373
- Ⓓ SE 658 380
- Ⓔ SE 658 384
- Ⓕ SE 665 380

Skipwith Common is one of the few remaining lowland heaths in northern England, a characteristic that once extended across much of the Vale of York. Left to itself, the area would revert to woodland dominated by birch, oak and pine, for it is, in fact, man-made; cleared by Bronze Age farmers and maintained in an open state by grazing and bracken clearance, with the wet areas exploited for peat and reeds. These habitats are a refuge for threatened flora and fauna, but traditional management by light grazing and tree felling is necessary to maintain a landscape that has existed for 3,500 years.

During World War Two, the area around King Rudding Farm was RAF Riccall, a heavy-bomber training station housing 32 Halifax aircraft and over 1,400 personnel. Although decommissioned in 1949, some dilapidated buildings, parts of the runway and dispersal areas, and the bomb store can still be seen.

One of the old peat ponds on Skipwith Common

Leave the rear of the car park beside a large gate onto a track across the common. Reaching a junction Ⓐ, bear left, walking 100m to a second junction. Keep left with the main track, ignoring side paths until you reach another prominent junction Ⓑ. Swing sharp left through

SCALE 1:25000 or 2½ INCHES to 1 MILE 4CM to 1KM

a kissing-gate and follow the path directly ahead, which circles past bomb storage bunkers. A boardwalk at the far end leads to a platform overlooking an old pond created by peat digging. After passing a memorial to the wartime personnel who served here, leave through the kissing-gate back to **B**. Take the track ahead through more woodland, later crossing a perimeter dispersal track and then a cattle grid.

Reaching a small car park **C**, turn right to a small gate at the rear. Head away; walking along the end of what was once the main runway. Go forward beyond its end on a path into trees, shortly curving right within the woodland edge. At a junction, keep left by the fence, later bending right before a battered oak. Stick with the winding perimeter path, eventually reaching a broad track. Follow it left, back past **A** to find, just beyond, a path marked off left.

Walk at the edge of the wood to a corner, there going left to a gate out of the reserve **D**. Walk forwards and then swing right over a bridged ditch. At the next corner, wind right and then left over Southfield Drain and continue beside the hedge. At the end, go right and left over a stile, crossing a final field to emerge onto a lane opposite the Old Vicarage **E**.

Turn right through Skipwith. Approaching the duck pond, the **Drovers Arms** lies to the left. The onward route, however, is right, going right again along Common Road. Leaving the village, cross a cattle grid onto the common. Just beyond, as the lane bends right **F**, leave left beside a redundant footbridge into the trees. Approaching a kissing-gate, swing right to follow a path beside a fence paralleling Blackwood Road. Through a gate, continue within an enclosure, moving right at the far end to find a gate in the corner back out to the car park. ●

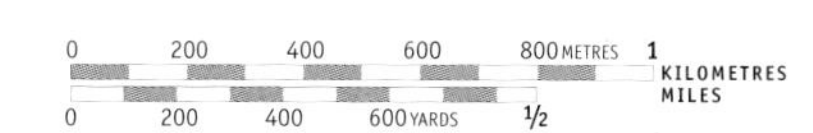

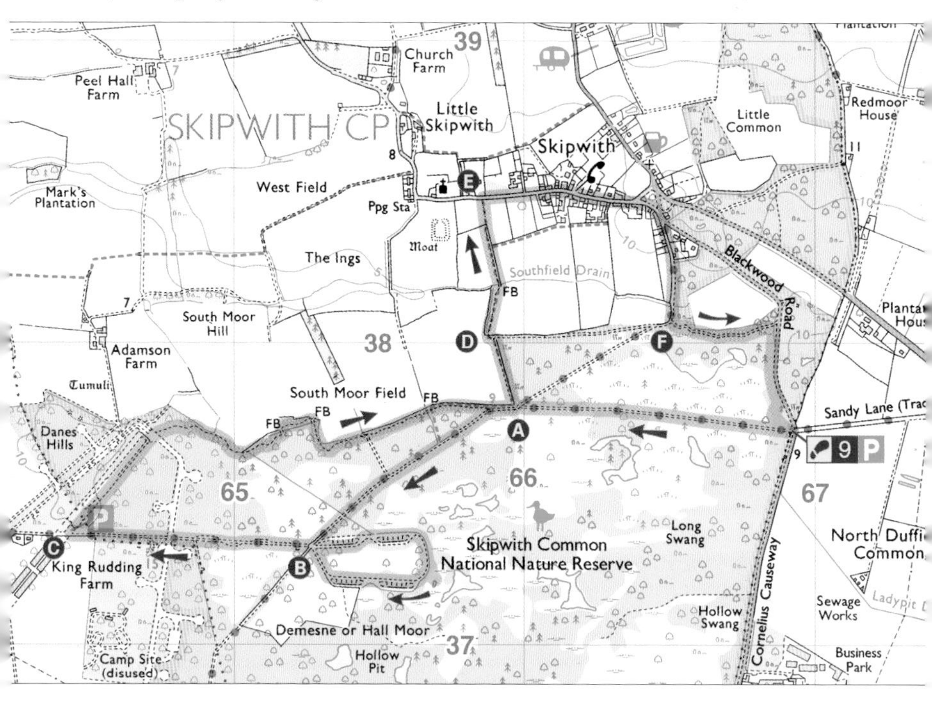

North Cliff and Filey Brigg

		GPS waypoints
Start	Filey, The Crescent. *Alternative start at North Cliff Country Park* Ⓔ	[start] TA 118 803
Distance	5 miles (8km). Shorter version starting from the Country Park, 4¼ miles (7km)	Ⓐ TA 120 808 Ⓑ TA 107 813 Ⓒ TA 110 824
Height gain	475 feet (145m). Shorter version 410 feet (125m)	Ⓓ TA 130 815 Ⓔ TA 120 813
Approximate time	2½ hours. Shorter version 2¼ hours	
Parking	Filey, or North Cliff Country Park	
Ordnance Survey maps	Landranger 101 (Scarborough), Explorer 301 (Scarborough, Bridlington & Flamborough Head)	

This is a straightforward route and includes some fine cliff walking that extends onto the promontory of Filey Brigg, offering superb coastal views across the sweeping curve of Filey Bay to Flamborough Head. Options include a shorter route omitting the town, which begins from North Cliff Country Park, and a short detour to Filey's medieval church.

With an extensive sandy beach and grand views to Flamborough Head, the arrival of the railway transformed the old fishing village of Filey into a popular Victorian resort. Despite the later Butlin's holiday camp, it retained throughout the years an air of gentility and elegance. Nowhere is this elegance more apparent than at The Crescent, one of the finest in the country and developed by John Wilkes Unett, a Birmingham solicitor, between 1835 and 1850.

[start] From the bandstand on The Crescent, follow the gardens north past the Roman Stones, found on Carr Naze after heavy rain in 1857 caused a landslide. Where the road bends inland at a sign to Coble Landing, keep ahead into a small park, from which a stepped path drops through terraced gardens to Cargate Hill. Follow it down to the sea front and turn left along the promenade to the slipway at Coble Landing Ⓐ. Keep with the main road as it swings inland into Church Ravine to climb past a telephone box – *where the shorter route joins*. Bear right at the top of the hill and then keep left past the road to the country park. At a roundabout, cross and follow the main road in the direction of Scarborough.

After ½ mile (800m), turn off right along a track to Filey Field Farm Ⓑ. Walk past the buildings and carry on along a path, rising gently at the field edge. At the top of the second field, swing left around the corner and then, after 50 yds go right. Resume the climb along the margin between open fields to the cliff path Ⓒ.

Turn right along North Cliff, where

breaks in the embankment afford spectacular views to the sea-washed rocks below. Farther on, Filey's Rocket Pole stands to the right. Representing the mast of a stricken ship, it was used by the Filey Volunteer Life Saving Rocket Company. One member would shin up while others would practice firing a rocket line for him to catch. Formed in 1872, the group was only disbanded in the 1960s when better navigation aids improved the safety of shipping.

At a prominent triangular stone marking the junction of the Yorkshire Wolds Way and Cleveland Way, take the path ahead that runs along Carr Naze. Dramatic crumbling cliffs buttress either side of the long, narrow peninsula, which at its tip falls dramatically to the low, wave-washed tongue of Filey Brigg that protrudes far beyond into the sea. The views are equally stunning in all directions and it is no surprise that it was used for a Roman signal station, one of five known along this section of coast. During the 4th century, the peninsula would have been much wider than today and the fort served to provide early warning of raiding parties from Scotland or across the North Sea.

From the end of the path **D**, retrace your steps to the marker stone and continue along the cliffs towards Filey. Reaching a car park, carry on along the grass strip above the cliffs to the edge of a deep wooded ravine, Wool Dale. *If you began from the country park, go right back to the café* **E**, *otherwise, you can*

SCALE 1:25 000 or 2½ INCHES to 1 MILE *4CM to 1KM*

continue down the steep, stepped path into the ravine, crossing the slipway road to climb back to the cliffs on the far side.

The shorter walk begins from the Country Park café E. *Cross the drive and walk past a children's play area and the coach park, following the southern rim of the ravine to the cliffs.*

Either way, follow the cliff path south towards Filey, from which St Oswald's Church can be seen over to the right. Approaching another wooded gully, the path drops a few steps to a junction. To visit the church, go right, alternatively, turn left and follow the zigzag path down through the trees to emerge at the foot of Church Ravine above Coble Landing A. *If you started from the café, turn right up the hill,* otherwise retrace your outward route through the town to the bandstand.

The Crescent at Filey

Ripon and the rivers Skell and Ure

Start	Ripon, Market Place
Distance	5½ miles (8.9km)
Height gain	165 feet (50m)
Approximate time	2½ hours
Parking	Ripon
Ordnance Survey maps	Landranger 99 (Northallerton & Ripon), Explorer 299 (Ripon & Boroughbridge)

GPS waypoints

- SE 312 712
- Ⓐ SE 313 709
- Ⓑ SE 332 702
- Ⓒ SE 330 704
- Ⓓ SE 323 719
- Ⓔ SE 317 719
- Ⓕ SE 318 709

From several points on this undemanding walk, there are distant views of Ripon Cathedral. There is much attractive walking through woodland and across meadows beside the banks of the rivers Skell and Ure, which meet just to the east of Ripon. The middle section is by way of fields and a track to the village of Sharow.

Elevated to the status of cathedral in 1836 – although even now, some maps still refer to it as 'minster' – the church at Ripon was founded by St Wilfrid in 672. It was sacked by the English king in 940, but the original crypt survives beneath the present building and is a remarkable example of early Saxon architecture. A second church was also destroyed, this time by William the Conqueror, and its successor was incorporated within the building we see today, begun by the then Archbishop of York, Roger de Pont l'Evêque in the 12th century. Amongst the treasures to be found are carvings of strange beasts in the choir, including one depicting a griffon chasing a couple of rabbits into their burrow. Some suggest that these inspired Lewis Carroll to write Alice in Wonderland, for he often visited Ripon to see his father who was a canon here in 1852.

The cathedral stands as an impressive focus to the attractive market town, where a bustling street market is still held every Thursday. The square is also the venue for two annual fairs, one on Spring Bank Holiday and the second to commemorate St Wilfrid, held on the Saturday preceding the first Monday in August. Both are colourful occasions with many events and side shows. Another ancient tradition, going back 900 years and still continued is that of the Wakeman, the night watchman employed to keep law and order in the town, who at 9 o'clock each evening, sounds his horn in the square.

The walk starts in the Market Place. Facing the 18th-century town hall, leave by the left corner along Kirkgate, keeping left with it to reach the cathedral. Turn right down Bedern Bank, walking ahead at the roundabout along King Street to cross a bridge over

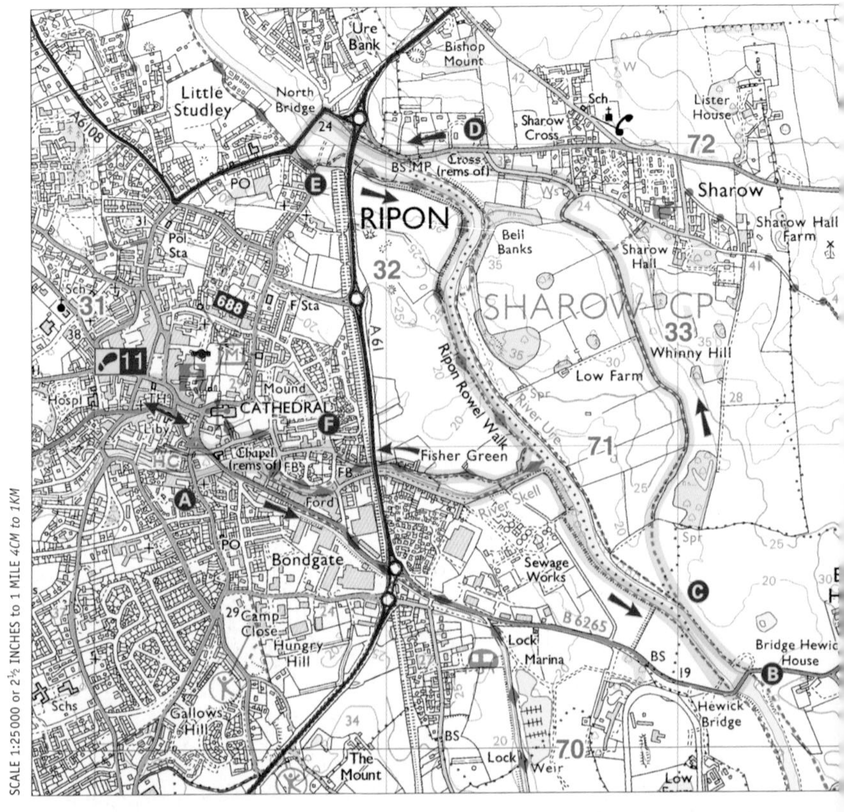

0 200 400 600 800 METRES 1 KILOMETRES
0 200 400 600 YARDS ½ MILES

the River Skell **A**.

Beyond, leave immediately along a riverside path on the left, passing the ancient Hospital and Church of St John the Baptist which were founded in 1109. Remain with the water beneath the next bridge to a riverside pub, **The Water Rat**, crossing the street there to return to the bank. Meeting another road, carry on beside the Skell along Fisher Green, passing under a former railway bridge, now carrying the bypass. At the end, continue ahead along a wooded path, which soon swings past the confluence with the Ure.

Emerging from the trees, cross the end of a track and walk on atop a low flood embankment and then at the edge of a field, ultimately emerging onto the road beside Hewick Bridge. Exercising caution since the road is narrow, cross the river and immediately leave the road for a path off left signed to Sharow **B**.

Dropping from the embankment, cross the end of a track to a ford and continue at the perimeter of the field by the river. After ¼ mile (400m), look out for a path bearing away through the crop **C** towards the left-hand edge of distant trees. Through a gate in the far hedge, turn right on another field boundary path that shortly falls right to continue below the hedge. Meeting the end of a farm track, follow it on for a little over ½ mile (800m), eventually winding around to emerge onto a lane in Sharow. Go left to a junction at Sharow Cross **D**. During the Middle Ages there were eight such crosses beside various roads into the town, each a mile (1.6km) from Ripon's church and defining the area in which sanctuary could be obtained.

Go left along Dishforth Road, but as you later approach a roundabout, bear off left along a footpath taking you beneath the bypass. Returning to the road beyond, go left and left again over North Bridge. On the other side, turn into Magdalen's Road, leaving on the bend through a kissing-gate to the left Ⓔ.

The ongoing way takes you back beneath the bypass, curving on through meadows bordering the Ure. Beyond a broken kissing-gate, pass through a clump of trees to continue on a more enclosed path. Eventually the way forks. Take the right branch, which bends around to run with the River Skell. At another split keep right at the edge of a rough meadow, rejoining the river at the far end to pass out through a kissing-gate onto a track.

To the left it leads back beneath the main road to become a street. Carry on to a double junction at its end Ⓕ, crossing ahead into Low Mill Road. Around a right-hand bend, take the first left, High Street Agnesgate and walk up beside the grounds below the cathedral. At the top go right and at the roundabout, right again, retracing your outward steps along Bedern Bank and back to the Market Square.

Ripon Cathedral

Welburn and Castle Howard

Start	Welburn, by the Crown and Cushion
Distance	5¾ miles (9.2km)
Height gain	360 feet (110m)
Approximate time	3 hours
Parking	Roadside parking at Welburn
Ordnance Survey maps	Landranger 100 (Malton & Pickering), Explorer 300 (Howardian Hills & Malton)

GPS waypoints

- Start: SE 720 680
- A: SE 722 692
- B: SE 719 706
- C: SE 732 694
- D: SE 730 687
- E: SE 723 679

Almost the whole of this walk is across the parkland and through the woodlands of the Castle Howard estate on the northern fringes of the Vale of York. Views of the great house and some of the other buildings that form part of the park's landscape are to be had, set against a backdrop of the Howardian Hills and the distant Yorkshire Wolds.

With the **Crown and Cushion** on your left, walk along Main Road and take the first left down Water Lane. Bear left at the end through a barrier and continue along a track in the direction of Coneysthorpe. Keep ahead at a junction towards woodland, where the path enters the trees and falls to cross a stream. Climb away beyond, emerging through a gate at the top of the wood. Carry on to reach a tarmac track **A**.

Go left but almost immediately, turn off right, heading down to New River Bridge, from which there is a good view upstream to Castle Howard.

Charles Howard, the third Earl of Carlisle began the building in 1699, employing the then unproved architect Vanbrugh and his able assistant Hawksmoor, a protégé of Wren. A century and three generations of Carlisles passed before it was finally completed and the park landscaped and set with grandiose follies in the fashion of the era. From the ornate bridge, you can see the Pyramid and Temple, while to the east is a great mausoleum, where the third Earl was finally laid to rest.

Climb away across the park over a rise, dropping on the far side to a three-way fingerpost by the corner of a fence. Still following signs to Coneysthorpe, go left joining a track beside a

The bridge over New River Pond

stone wall. Through a gate bear off left at the edge of trees to a junction **B**.

Walk right, shortly crossing Mill Hills Beck before rising into more woodland and another junction by Bog Hall Farm. Signed right towards Gaterley, the ongoing track weaves left and right between the buildings to continue beyond at the edge of fields. Eventually reaching another farm at Low Gaterley, turn right in front of a barn and head uphill to reach a tarmac drive **C**.

Walk right for a little over ½ mile (800m) to meet your outward route at **A**. Briefly retrace your steps to the wood cloaking East Moor Banks. Go through the gate but now turn left at a signpost to Crambeck, following a path that wanders within the trees along the top of the bank. After ½ mile (800m), look for a path signed off to the right **D**. It is just before a small clearing where stands another of the estate's whimsical monuments, a pillar aptly called Four Faces.

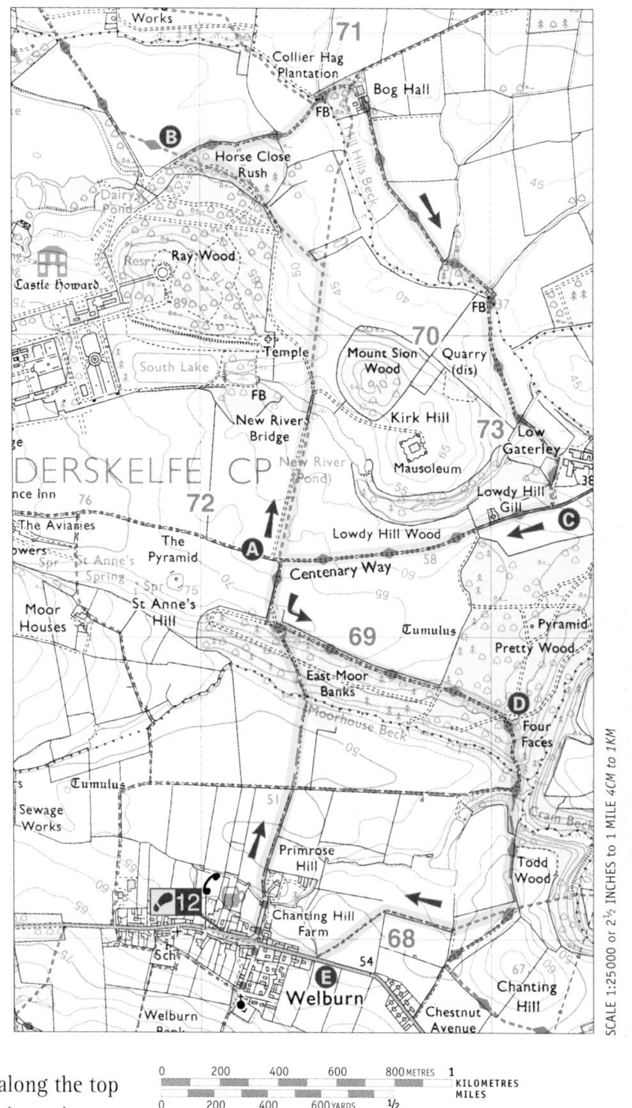

The path descends through the trees to recross Moorhouse Beck. Over a stile, walk on to a junction and keep ahead on a bridleway, marked towards Welburn. Leaving the wood through a gate, carry on beside a field to another gate. Bear right with the bridleway, but at a fork, just a few yards farther on, branch right on a footpath, still following signs to Welburn. The trod strikes across rough pasture towards the distant spire of Welburn's church. At the far side, keep ahead through a gap along the edge of a field. At the corner, strike a left diagonal across a final field to emerge onto the lane at the edge of the village **E**. Turn right back to the starting point.

Newbald Wold

Start	North Newbald
Distance	5¾ miles (9.25km)
Height gain	590 feet (180m)
Approximate time	3 hours
Parking	North Newbald, around the Green
Ordnance Survey maps	Landranger 106 (Market Weighton), Explorer 293 (Kingston upon Hull & Beverley)

GPS waypoints

- Start: SE 912 367
- A: SE 912 369
- B: SE 908 383
- C: SE 928 395
- D: SE 927 379
- E: SE 925 373
- F: SE 926 369

Almost the whole of the walk is in open country, providing extensive views, both across the wolds and the Vale of York. The route crests a shoulder of Newbald Wold and then rises along a dry valley onto its summit, the return dipping into neighbouring Swin Dale.

Pevsner described the church, as 'the most complete Norman church in the East Riding', while the whipping post on the village green is claimed to be the last used in Britain for a public flogging.

From the **Tiger Inn**, follow the main street, Ratten Row past the village's second pub, **The Gnu**, a play on words for it was formerly The New Inn. Bend right as it becomes Galegate, but then at a sharp left bend, turn off into Townside Road. Just before Townside Close, leave left onto a farm drive **A**.

Where the drive swings to Dot Hill Farm, keep ahead on a grass track over the shoulder of the hill and continue down the field edge to the bottom by Syke House Farm **B**.

To the right a path leads along the base of the dale – ignore the gate on

Near North Newbald

the right a short way along. Climbing gently, pass through a couple of kissing-gates and later side step a wood, eventually meeting the Yorkshire Wolds Way at Gare Gate C.

A sign directs you right along a hedged track to Hessle, climbing over the brow where a triangulation pillar marks the high point. Reaching a lane, walk right, heading downhill some 200 yds to find a track dropping left towards South Cave D.

Emerging at the bottom onto another lane by a farm, go right. After 350 yds, turn off left again with the Yorkshire Wolds Way E, passing through a gate into the head of Swin Dale. The track later swings left, but very soon after, look for a path across the crop field on the right F, which strikes to a fingerpost below the wood at the far side. The ongoing path winds up through the trees, breaking out at the top in the corner of a field. Carry on along its right margin to reach a lane and follow it right, back down into the village.

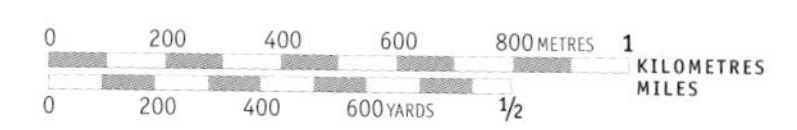

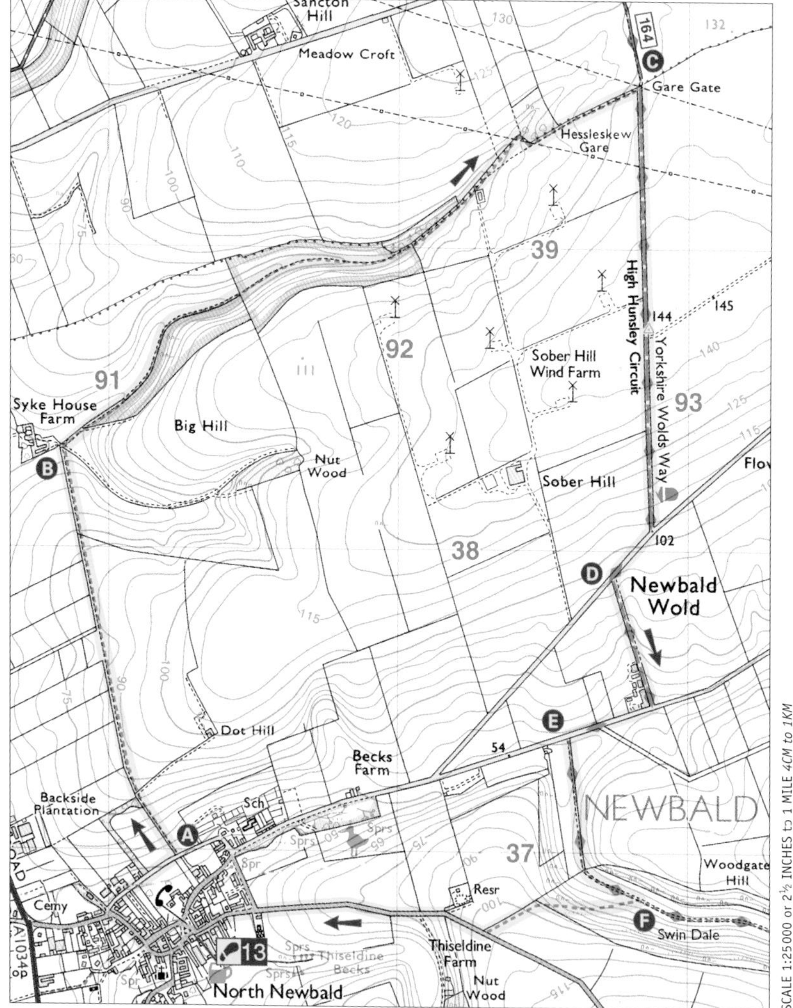

SCALE 1:25 000 or 2½ INCHES to 1 MILE *4CM to 1KM*

Fridaythorpe and Huggate

Start	Fridaythorpe
Distance	7 miles (11.2km)
Height gain	720 feet (220m)
Approximate time	3½ hours
Parking	Roadside parking at Fridaythorpe, near the church
Ordnance Survey maps	Landranger 106 (Market Weighton), Explorer 294 (Market Weighton & Yorkshire Wolds Central)

GPS waypoints

- SE 874 592
- Ⓐ SE 874 584
- Ⓑ SE 862 569
- Ⓒ SE 881 557
- Ⓓ SE 882 550
- Ⓔ SE 884 575

This outstanding walk explores a classic high wolds landscape of open hillsides and steep-sided, narrow dales with extensive and superb views, much of it following the well-waymarked Yorkshire Wolds Way. The attractive villages of Fridaythorpe and Huggate both have interesting churches and appealing pubs, and the brief detour into Huggate is definitely recommended.

The highest village on the Yorkshire Wolds, Fridaythorpe's unusual name has nothing to do with the anticipation of an approaching weekend, but instead betrays the settlement's 9th-century Scandinavian origins as the homestead of Frigda. The tiny church, tucked behind cottages at the start may claim even earlier foundation, with an intriguing inscription 'This 713 found hear' [sic] on a column of the arcade. However, the zigzag carving on the doorway and chancel arch is undoubtedly Norman. An unusual feature is the clock staring from the tower, said to be styled on one found in a French château and reminding us of our mortality with the warning 'Time is short, eternity is long'.

From the church, follow the street through the village to the main road. Go right, crossing to take the second turning left, signed as the Yorkshire Wolds Way to Huggate. It later degrades to a track, shortly reaching a fork Ⓐ.

Bear right, but leave almost immediately through a gate on the left by a Yorkshire Wolds Way signpost. Instead of following the obvious grass track downhill, turn right and stay high beside the fence, from which there is a striking view along Holm Dale. Beyond a gate and stile, a field track develops that winds across successive fields, eventually leading to Wold House Farm. Keep ahead through the farmyard and then go left in front of a barn into a second yard. Walk to the far side by the farmhouse and leave right along the access track.

After 350 yds look for a waypost at the end of a hedge on the left Ⓑ. The path dogs its right flank, dropping to a gate at the bottom corner. Veering slightly right, continue through a

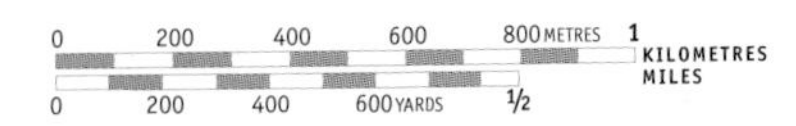

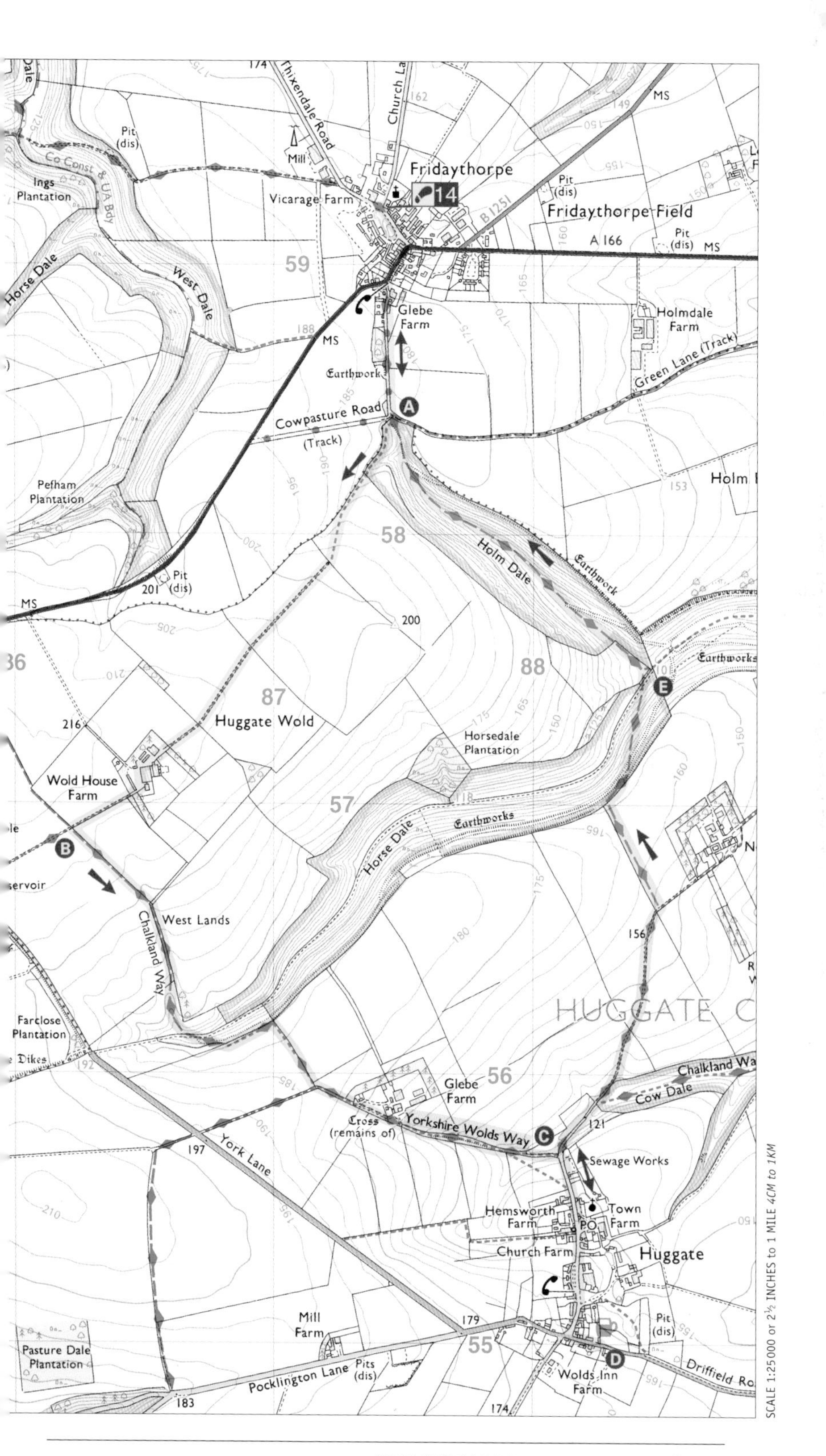
Fridaythorpe
Fridaythorpe Field
Vicarage Farm
Mill
Thixendale Road
Church La
Ings Plantation
Co Const & UA Bdy
Horse Dale
West Dale
Glebe Farm
Holmdale Farm
Green Lane (Track)
Earthwork
Cowpasture Road
(Track)
Pefham Plantation
Holm Dale
Earthworks
Huggate Wold
Wold House Farm
Horsedale Plantation
Horse Dale
West Lands
Chalkland Way
Farclose Plantation
HUGGATE
Glebe Farm
Cross (remains of)
Yorkshire Wolds Way
Cow Dale
Sewage Works
York Lane
Hemsworth Farm
Town Farm
Church Farm
Huggate
Mill Farm
Pocklington Lane
Pasture Dale Plantation
Wolds Inn Farm
Driffield Ro
A 166
B 1251
SCALE 1:25 000 or 2½ INCHES to 1 MILE 4CM to 1KM

Horse Dale

shallow fold into Horse Dale. Bear left to a waymarked gate and, maintaining the same slanting course, climb the opposite hillside. The path levels along a grass terrace and gives a splendid prospect along the dale. Captivating it might be, but do not miss a gate up on the right, some 150 yds along through which you should pass. Head away at the field edge to meet a track at the far side. Back with the Yorkshire Wolds Way, follow it left to Glebe Farm. As it swings into the farm, leave ahead along an enclosed path to bypass the buildings. Rejoining the track beyond, follow it down to meet a lane **C**.

Huggate lies to the right, the lane climbing past the church into the village. You will find **The Wolds Inn** at the far end, just to the left along the main road **D**.

Return to **C**, but now carry on down to cross the head of Cow Dale, rising with the ongoing farm lane onto the wold. After ½ mile (800m), where it curves right to begin its descent to Northfield House, abandon the lane beside a Yorkshire Wolds Way signpost for a field-edge path on the left. Through a gate at the far end, the way angles right, dropping into Horse Dale. Follow the bottom fence right to a stile beside a gate on your left **E**.

Walk away along the foot of Holm Dale, gradually climbing to a fork near the head of the valley. Take the right branch, from which there is a final pull to a gate at the top by point **A**. Follow your outward route back into Fridaythorpe.

Watton and Kilnwick

Start	Watton, the Green at the corner of the main road and village street
Distance	6¾ miles (11km)
Height gain	115 feet (35m)
Approximate time	3½ hours
Parking	By the Green at Watton
Ordnance Survey maps	Landranger 106 (Market Weighton), Explorers 294 (Market Weighton & Yorkshire Wolds Central) and 295 (Bridlington, Driffield & Hornsea)

GPS waypoints

- TA 018 500
- A TA 016 498
- B SE 997 497
- C SE 994 503
- D TA 002 513
- E TA 019 514
- F TA 024 512
- G TA 021 499

This walk lies on the eastern fringes of the Yorkshire Wolds chalk beside clear-flowing becks and through pleasant woodland as well as offering open views from the higher country. The way passes two secluded village churches, one standing on the site of a now-vanished medieval monastery.

From the main road, head into the village, but turn left after 150 yds along a drive between the houses. Through a kissing-gate at the end, strike across grazing to another kissing-gate. Walk past the front of a cottage to cross Watton Beck A.

Turn right beside it along a low embankment, shortly entering a wood. Ignore a bridge across the stream, following the path as it later swings away through reeds and then thicket to a bridge over Kilnwick Beck. Breaking into open ground, turn right along the field edge and continue into the next field. About halfway along, look for a

Kilnwick church

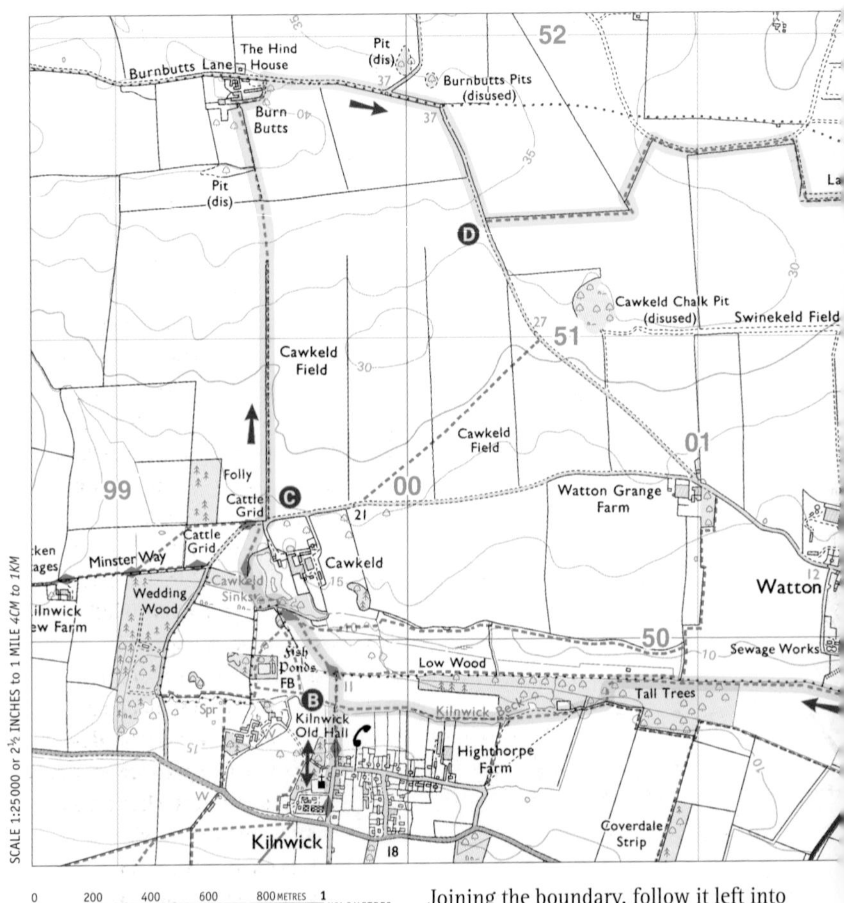

footbridge back across the stream into the trees. A path winds through to emerge in the corner of another field. Walk ahead by its left edge to reach a four-way fingerpost towards the far end **B**.

Kilnwick lies just to the left, its brick and stone church particularly interesting for the Norman carving surmounting the doorway. To reach it, go to the end of the track and turn right through the gates of Glebe House. The drive winds around to the church.

Return to point **B** and follow the Minster Way across the width of the field. Over a footbridge, cross into the next field and bear left towards a wood. Joining the boundary, follow it left into the very corner, where a stile and plank bridge take the way into the wood. Wind through the trees to emerge into another meadow and keep going beside the right-hand boundary. Where that later swings away, keep ahead to a narrow lane at the far side. Follow it right past a cattle-grid but then abandon the lane in favour of a waymarked track on the left **C**.

At the end of the field, pass through a hedge gap. Go a few steps left and then swing right to strike across, keeping ahead as you later join a boundary. Approaching a farm, follow the hedge around to the right, skirting the buildings and yard to come out on a lane.

Go right and then, at a junction,

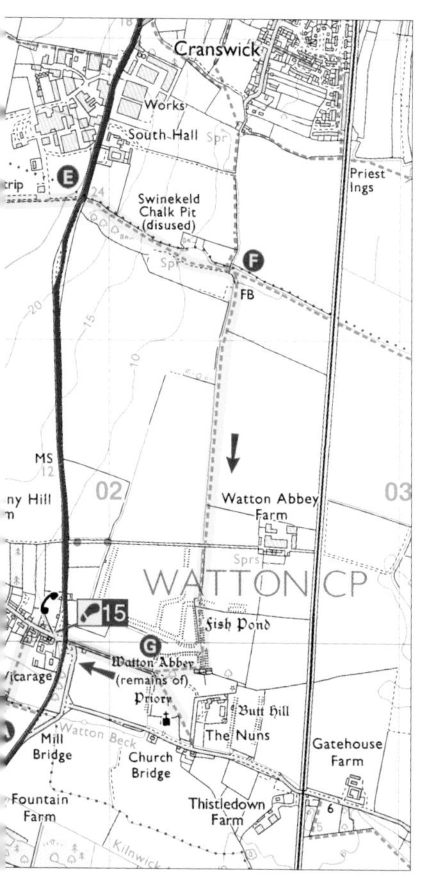

keep ahead with the minor lane. About 400 yds beyond a bend, turn off through a kissing-gate on the left **D**. Head away along the margin between open fields, in a while angling round to intercept a concrete track. Go right and, at a junction, right again, staying with the track as it later swings sharply left. The way runs beside a grass landing strip before leaving through gates near a small agricultural workshop onto a road **E**.

Cross to a kissing-gate opposite and follow a grass track beside the edge of rough grazing. At the far end, ignore a footbridge on the left, walking a few yards farther on to a signpost beside a redundant kissing-gate **F**. Leave the track there, turning right across a small patch of rough ground to a kissing-gate. Cross a drain and continue along a field-edge path alongside a drain on the right.

Later, keep ahead over a crossing concrete track, making for farm buildings on the site of Watton Abbey. The ditches and mounds in the fields on either side mark old fishponds and outbuildings of the monastery.

Founded in 1150 for the Gilbertine order, it contained separate houses for canons and nuns. Although the rules supposedly offered no opportunity for the sexes to mix, there were occasional scandals of pregnancies. The story of the 12th-century Nun of Watton, however, is particularly brutal for the retribution meted out. She had been placed there as a child but had little enthusiasm for the calling and developed a relationship with a lay brother. When her condition became apparent, the other nuns castrated her lover and she was savagely beaten and incarcerated. However, she had a vision of the Archbishop of York, who cleansed her soul and body; the pregnancy 'disappeared' and the chains fell away. Aelred of Rievaulx subsequently investigated the matter and proclaimed a miracle, although even now there are stories of a ghostly nun wandering the grounds.

Reaching a ruined brick barn, turn right beside it to leave the field through a kissing-gate. Walk past the building and keep ahead to another kissing-gate at the far side of the field **G**.

Before going through, however, take a short detour to see Watton's church, which lies back across the field to the left. Make for the corner of the hedge beyond its eastern end to find a gate into the churchyard. Retrace your steps to the kissing-gate **G** and finally follow the enclosed path out to the main road opposite the village.

Flamborough Head

Start	Flamborough Head, South Landing, signposted from Flamborough
Distance	7 miles (11.3km)
Height gain	755 feet (230m)
Approximate time	3½ hours
Parking	South Landing
Ordnance Survey maps	Landranger 101 (Scarborough), Explorer 301 (Scarborough, Bridlington & Flamborough Head)

GPS waypoints

- Start: TA 230 695
- A TA 230 693
- B TA 253 707
- C TA 238 719
- D TA 233 719
- E TA 231 712
- F TA 227 705

After an exhilarating walk along the dramatic chalk cliffs of Flamborough Head, the walk turns across the neck of the headland to pass through the attractive village of Flamborough. There are occasional short steep descents and climbs along the way, but in compensation the views are magnificent.

Leaving the car park, follow the wooded lane down to South Landing **A**. Just before the lifeboat station, drop left and climb the stepped path out of the base of the valley onto the headland. Follow the path right and then left, shortly reaching a fork by a sculpture representing St Oswald, the patron saint of fishermen.

Take the right branch and carry on along the coast. Glancing back, there is a view to Bridlington, while in front across the headland are the towers of two generations of lighthouse. Later, ignore a footpath signed off towards Lighthouse Road and continue to the tip of Flamborough Head.

Approaching the fog signal station and radio masts, the path forks at a waypost, offering a choice of routes either side of an open grassy swathe. Both lead to a tarmac track from the signal station. Follow it left towards the lighthouse.

Just before the lighthouse **B**, bear off right onto a path below its seaward wall. Meeting a road, keep right along the cliff top past the car park to a topograph. It shows, among other things, that Flamborough Head is equidistant from John O'Groats and Lands End – 362 miles (582km).

Bear right to continue along the clifftop path, from which there are dramatic views into the deep bays below, while inland across the golf course rises the slightly leaning octagonal chalk tower. It was built in 1669 by Sir John Clayton, and is the oldest light tower to survive in England. However, despite the dangers of this stretch of coast, it was apparently never used for its intended purpose and it was not until the 'new' tower was built in 1806 that a warning light shone from the point.

The path eventually curves in above North Landing, where a track leads down to the beach **C**. Cross and carry on along the seaward edge of the car

SCALE 1:27 777 or about 2¼ INCHES to 1 MILE 3.6CM to 1KM

park, from which the way is signed over a stile to Thornwick Bay. The path immediately drops steeply into a gully to cross a stream, rising more easily on the opposite side. Walking on, there is a fine picture back into North Landing and then later, the view ahead is of the perpendicular cliffs to the north. Approaching Thornwick, the path winds in above the head of the bay, finally dropping down a few steps to meet another path rising along the ravine. Follow it up left to join a track D.

Cross to a path opposite signed to Flamborough, which follows the field edge before becoming enclosed on its approach to Thornwick Farm. Turn left in front of the house, passing beside a white gate. At the corner of the walled garden go right and then swing left onto a drive in front of the shops and a bar serving the caravan site. Cross the main drive beside the security cabin and barrier to a short contained path and continue beyond at the edge of an open grass field. Meeting a lane at the far side Ⓔ, follow it right. Where it subsequently bends past a junction, keep ahead along a street into the centre of Flamborough village.

Carry on forward into Dog and Duck Square where, opposite the **Royal Dog and Duck**, you should turn left along Allison Lane. At the end Ⓕ, go right and keep ahead at a crossroads, following the ongoing lane back to the car park above South Landing.

Flamborough Head

Harpham, Burton Agnes and Kilham

		GPS waypoints
Start	Bracey Bridge picnic site, off A614 between Driffield and Burton Agnes	TA 076 619
Distance	7½ miles (12.2km)	Ⓐ TA 082 612
Height gain	230 feet (70m)	Ⓑ TA 092 617
Approximate time	3½ hours	Ⓒ TA 102 629
Parking	Bracey Bridge picnic site	Ⓓ TA 099 634
Ordnance Survey maps	Landranger 101 (Scarborough), Explorer 295 (Bridlington, Driffield & Hornsea)	Ⓔ TA 087 634
		Ⓕ TA 071 645
		Ⓖ TA 064 643

This walk across subtly undulating country links three attractive villages that lie at the foot of the wolds. All have pubs and medieval churches and there are extensive views from the gentle slopes. The route passes by Burton Agnes Hall, a fine Elizabethan mansion well worth a visit.

Begin over a stile beside a gate at the western end of the lay-by and head south on a track through a belt of trees. Before reaching Bracey Bridge Mill, branch off right onto a grass track, passing through a gate to continue at the edge of a large field. Mount a stile at the end by a sign to Lowthorpe and carry on across grazing. Leave over a stile beside a gate at the far side onto another track Ⓐ.

Go left, soon crossing a bridge over Lowthorpe Beck. Beyond a strip of wood walk past West End Farm, the track leaving through gates onto a lane. Turn right and keep ahead past a junction through Harpham to a cross-roads at the other end of the village. The church is to the right, but the route lies left in the direction of Bridlington. After 50 yds and just before the old chapel, look for a path disappearing over a stile on the right Ⓑ.

It leads through to the fields behind. Heading slightly left, strike out across the crop. Over another stile at the far side, continue the bearing to join a hedge and carry on with it on your left until you reach a waymarked stile. Cross and walk out on a right diagonal towards a pole, continuing along the line set by the overhead power cables. Over a bridged ditch and stile keep ahead at the edge of the next field for 50 yds to another stile. Beyond that, head half right towards the buildings of Burton Agnes, crossing another intervening stile before leaving over a final stile beside a gate near the top corner of the field onto the main road. Go right into the village to a junction opposite **The Blue Bell** Ⓒ. The walk continues up the lane, but it is worth first making a detour to see Burton Agnes Hall and the nearby St Martin's Church. In which case, carry on along

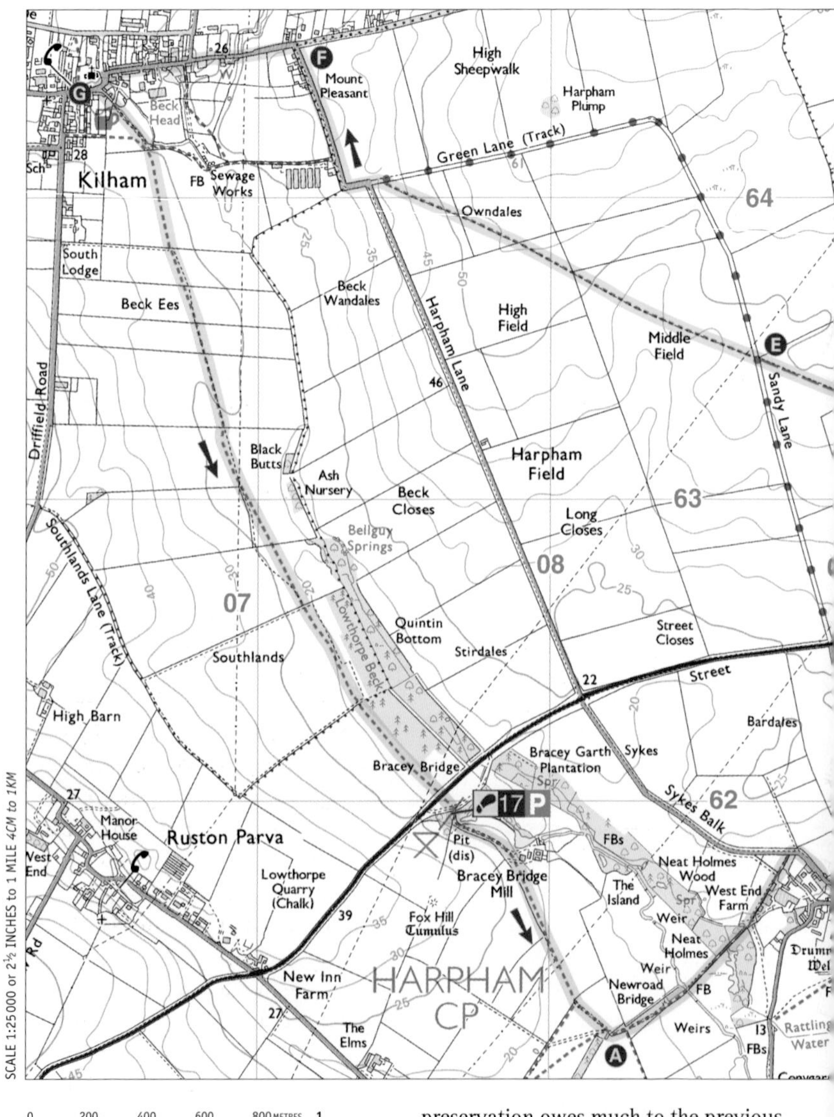

the main road a little farther to a crossroads by the village pond and there turn left. The hall is then off on the right and the church, approached along a tunnel of 300-year old yews, is at the end.

Built around a Norman manor house, Burton Agnes is one of the finest Elizabethan halls in the country. It has undergone little alteration and its preservation owes much to the previous owner, Marcus Wickham-Boynton, who began an extensive programme of restoration, creating a setting in which to house his growing collection of modern works of art.

Return to Ⓒ and now take the lane out of the village towards Rudston. After 1/4 mile (400m), turn off through a gap on the left Ⓓ. Walk away beside the left hedge, continuing beyond its end across a dip to a gap in the distant hedge. Through that, bear slightly right

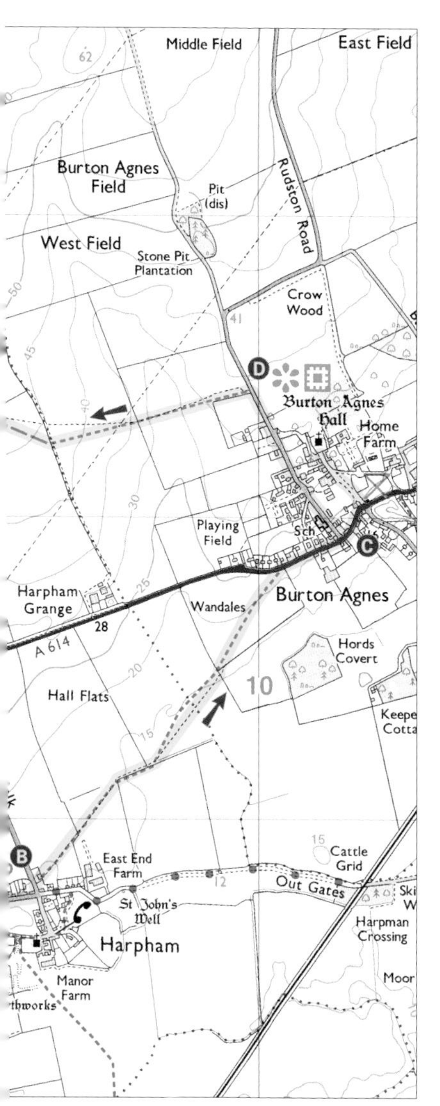

up the next field to pass beneath power cables, aiming for a tight clump of sycamore beside a waymarked gap in the top boundary. Maintain the diagonal across the next two fields and leave over a stile by a gate at the far side onto a rough tarmac track, Sandy Lane **E**.

Over the stile opposite, strike half-right across the field to the far corner. Keep the same direction across successive fields, eventually dropping out onto another track. Go left onto the

The church and Norman House at Burton Agnes Hall

corner of a lane. Walk ahead and follow it right winding through another bend, eventually arriving at a T-junction **F**. Keep with the main lane, walking past a second junction into the centre of Kilham. Curve left in front of the church, but as the lane then swings right, immediately turn off sharp left into Bakehouse Lane **G**.

Where that bends, go ahead over a stile beside a gate and head across a rough field to the far-left corner. There, ignore the lower gate and path off to the left and instead, walk forward through a broad gap into the next field. Keep ahead, maintaining the same line across a succession of fields. Later joining a hedge, bear slightly left from it to pass through the end boundary below the corner. Carry on across more fields to meet the out-jutting corner of a poplar plantation. Continue at its edge, climbing an embankment at the far end onto the main road opposite the Bracey Bridge picnic site. ●

Sheriff Hutton and Mowthorpe Hill

Start	Sheriff Hutton, crossroads in village centre
Distance	7½ miles (12.2km)
Height gain	525 feet (160m)
Approximate time	3½ hours
Parking	Roadside parking at Sheriff Hutton
Ordnance Survey maps	Landranger 100 (Malton & Pickering), Explorer 300 (Howardian Hills & Malton)

GPS waypoints

- Start SE 650 663
- A SE 659 667
- B SE 666 673
- C SE 674 699
- D SE 686 990
- E SE 679 676
- F SE 673 676

A walk across fields at the foot of the Howardian Hills is followed by an easy ascent onto Mowthorpe Hill, from where there are extensive views over the northern part of the Vale of York. After descending, the return leg follows a more undulating route, and on the final stretch the church and ruined castle at Sheriff Hutton stand out prominently on the low ridge occupied by the village.

The quiet village of Sheriff Hutton is dominated by the gaunt ruins of a 14th-century castle that belonged to the powerful Neville family. Richard Neville, Earl of Warwick, played a major role in the Wars of the Roses, and his daughter married Richard III. Their son, Edward Prince of Wales died in 1481 when only 11 years old and there is an alabaster memorial to him in the church of St Helen and Holy Cross.

Starting from the crossroads in the centre of the village by **The Highwayman**, walk along Main Street in the direction of the church. Keep ahead past the village's second pub, **The Castle**, but then bear left along East End, which ends in a small yard. Pass through to a gate at the far side and turn left at the field edge, continuing ahead beyond a corner to reach a lane Ⓐ.

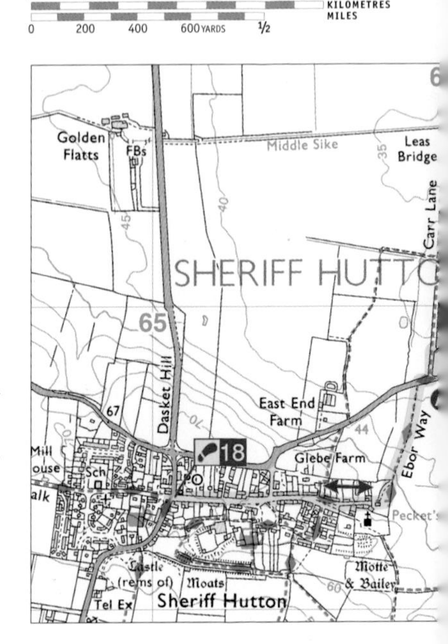

Go right and immediately left along a track, Carr Lane, but after only a few yards abandon it through a gateway on the right into a field. Stick with the right-hand hedge, leaving in the corner through a gate to go over a footbridge. Cross a training gallop and walk on beside a hedge on your right to meet a track at the far side **B**.

To the left it runs dead straight across the flat apron of fields below the edge of the Howardian Hills. Follow it

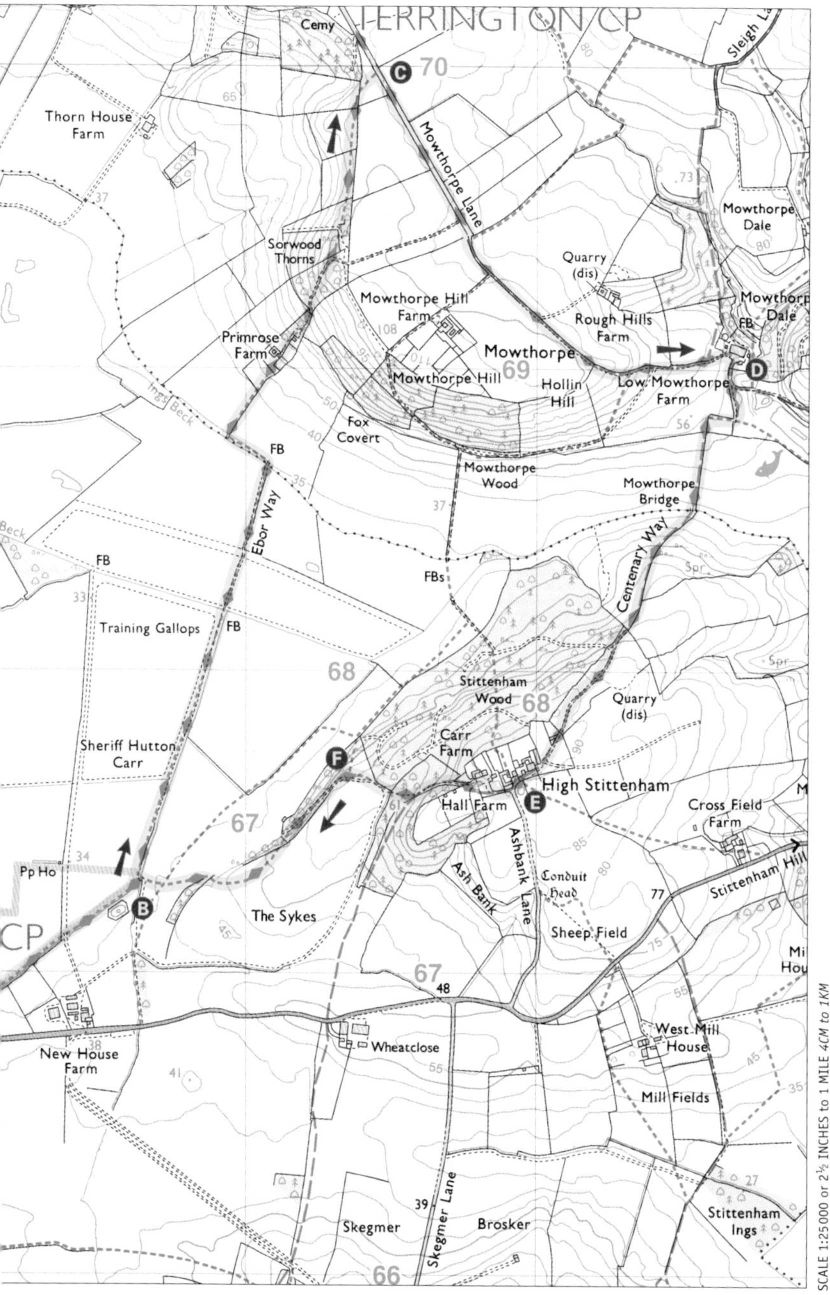

SCALE 1:25000 or 2½ INCHES to 1 MILE *4CM to 1KM*

Sheriff Hutton church

for almost a mile (1.6km), crossing one brook to reach a second, Ings Beck. Over that, turn left beside it, passing through a gap in the corner. Go right, accompanying the hedge up through a couple of fields to a house, Primrose Farm. Wind around out of the field and pass right of the farm to leave along its drive. Climb the hill to a sharp right-hand bend.

The ongoing track runs directly out to Mowthorpe Lane, saving you ½ mile (800m), but for a superb panorama across the Vale of York, take the waymarked gate on the left. Strike half-right through a plantation of saplings, leaving at the far corner onto the bend of a track. Cross to a trod contouring below more young trees, soon moving right to emerge onto another track. Through a gate to the left, the view opens across the plain, with York some 12 miles (19.3km) away to the south-east. Continue through two more gates, after which turn through a gate on the right. Bear left across a field to a final gate to reach Mowthorpe Lane **C**.

Go right, shortly passing the point at which the track from Primrose Farm emerges. A little farther on, where the main lane bends right, keep ahead on a track that eventually descends to Low Mowthorpe Farm. Bear right past barns to the farmhouse, just before which is a gate on the right **D**.

Through that, when the tarmac swings left to fishing ponds, walk ahead on a grass track to reach a gate on the right from which a bridleway is signed to High Stittenham. Cross to a second gate and then turn downhill at the edge of a couple of fields to Mowthorpe Bridge. On the far bank, climb away beside the boundary, passing through a gate at the top to continue on a track over the brow of the hill. Through a gate, carry on past cottages to a junction by Hall Farm **E**.

The track ahead, signed to Sheriff Hutton winds round to a junction in front of a converted barn. Turn left through a gate to reach a pair of adjacent gates. Go through the right-hand one and follow a descending path through a young plantation. Take the right branch at a fork soon emerging onto the edge of a field. Follow the bottom boundary of the wood a few yards right to a slight corner and there strike left across the field corner to a gate at the far side **F**.

Entering more trees, the path undulates to the left, but look out for a later waymark directing you back up the slope and over a stile into the field above. Go right, but as the boundary then curves up to the left, side-step into the adjacent field, walking a short distance past trees to a waypost. Veer away on a path across the crop to join a track at the far side. Follow it ahead through a broad gap in the hedge to return to point **B**. Bear off left at the field edge and retrace your outward route across the fields to Sheriff Hutton.

Hunmanby, Muston and Stocking Dale

Start	Hunmanby
Distance	7½ miles (12.1km)
Height gain	490 feet (150m)
Approximate time	3½ hours
Parking	Hunmanby
Ordnance Survey maps	Landranger 101 (Scarborough), Explorer 301 (Scarborough, Bridlington & Flamborough Head)

GPS waypoints

- Start: TA 095 774
- A: TA 105 794
- B: TA 094 797
- C: TA 074 782
- D: TA 070 759
- E: TA 088 775

This enjoyable walk links the pleasant villages of Hunmanby and Muston, which lie at the northerly edge of the Yorkshire Wolds overlooking Filey and the North Sea. The gentle chalk slopes afford splendid views across the open countryside, but perhaps the most idyllic section falls along the secluded wooded valley of Stocking Dale below Folkton Wold.

The village of Hunmanby appears in the *Domesday Book* as 'Hundemanebi' – meaning 'settlement of the Houndsman'. Among the village's assets were credited 'one church and one priest', although the present building dates mainly from the 12th century. Hunmanby grew as a successful market town and it was only after the arrival of the railway in the mid-19th century that nearby Filey gained precedence as the local centre.

Head uphill from the church and White Swan and, where the road shortly bends left, turn right into Castle Hill

The village of Hunmanby

and then immediately left into Northgate. Walk down to a sharp bend and keep ahead on a farm track, which leads to North Moor Farm. Ignore a gate at the end, and instead follow a contained path to its right that finishes through a kissing-gate into a field. Walk directly across to a gate and stile at the far side, where another track begins. Carry on at the field edge and over another stile, the track undulating gently on to emerge at a roundabout junction **A**.

Take the road left towards Scarborough, crossing to a pavement on its other side. Before long, cross back and take the turning to Muston, remaining with the main road as it winds through the village, passing the **Ship Inn**. At the far end of the village, just before the speed derestriction sign, leave through a gate on the left signed the Yorkshire Wolds Way **B**.

Parallel the road for 200 yds to another signpost and then swing left to rise gently away at the edge of successive pastures. Eventually emerging over a stile into a crop field the path strikes across to a gap in the far hedge. Pass through and turn left along a flower-rich field margin, walking over the wold and eventually emerging onto a lane **C**.

Take the track opposite to Stockendale Farm. Continuing past the farm, it curves to follow the right-hand edge of the field beyond. At a junction of tracks, keep ahead beside a belt of trees dropping to a wooded dip. There, the path swings left along the bottom edge of the field. At the bottom corner, carry on ahead into trees, the ongoing path gently falling along the base of Stocking Dale.

Beyond a gate, the path shortly breaks out onto the edge of pasture. Reaching a three-way signpost at the confluence with Camp Dale, keep ahead along the main valley, now following the Centenary Way. After crossing a stile the way continues beside a field. At the far side, join a track to climb the flank of the dale. Nearing the top, turn off left onto a grass track **D**.

Undulating easily across the high ground, there are impressive views across Fleming Dale. The track leads to a clump of trees sheltering Field House Farm. Walk into the yard, but then turn

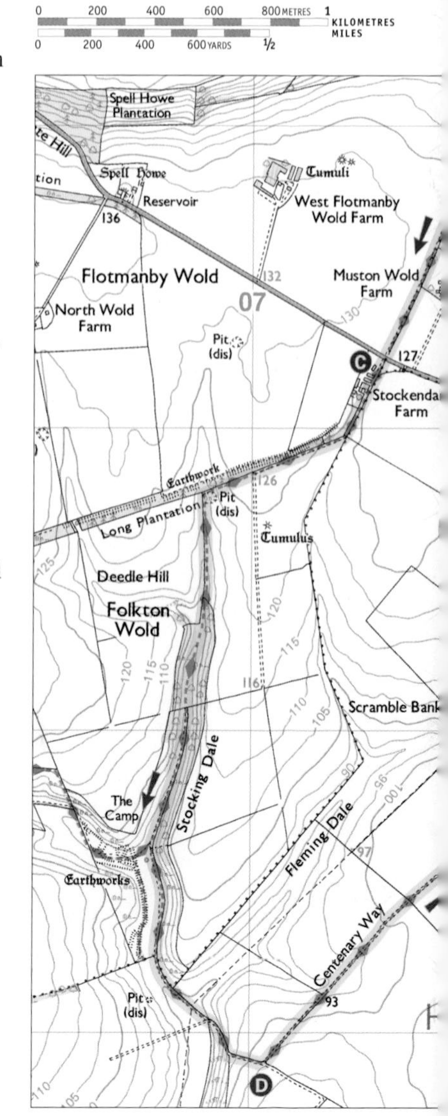

right between the first and second barns. Reaching the edge of the field, go left past the remaining barns and the farmhouse. Joining the farm's access drive, follow it out to the lane E.

Turn right, heading back towards Hunmanby. Go forward at a mini-roundabout and follow the main lane around to the right down Church Hill to return to the start.

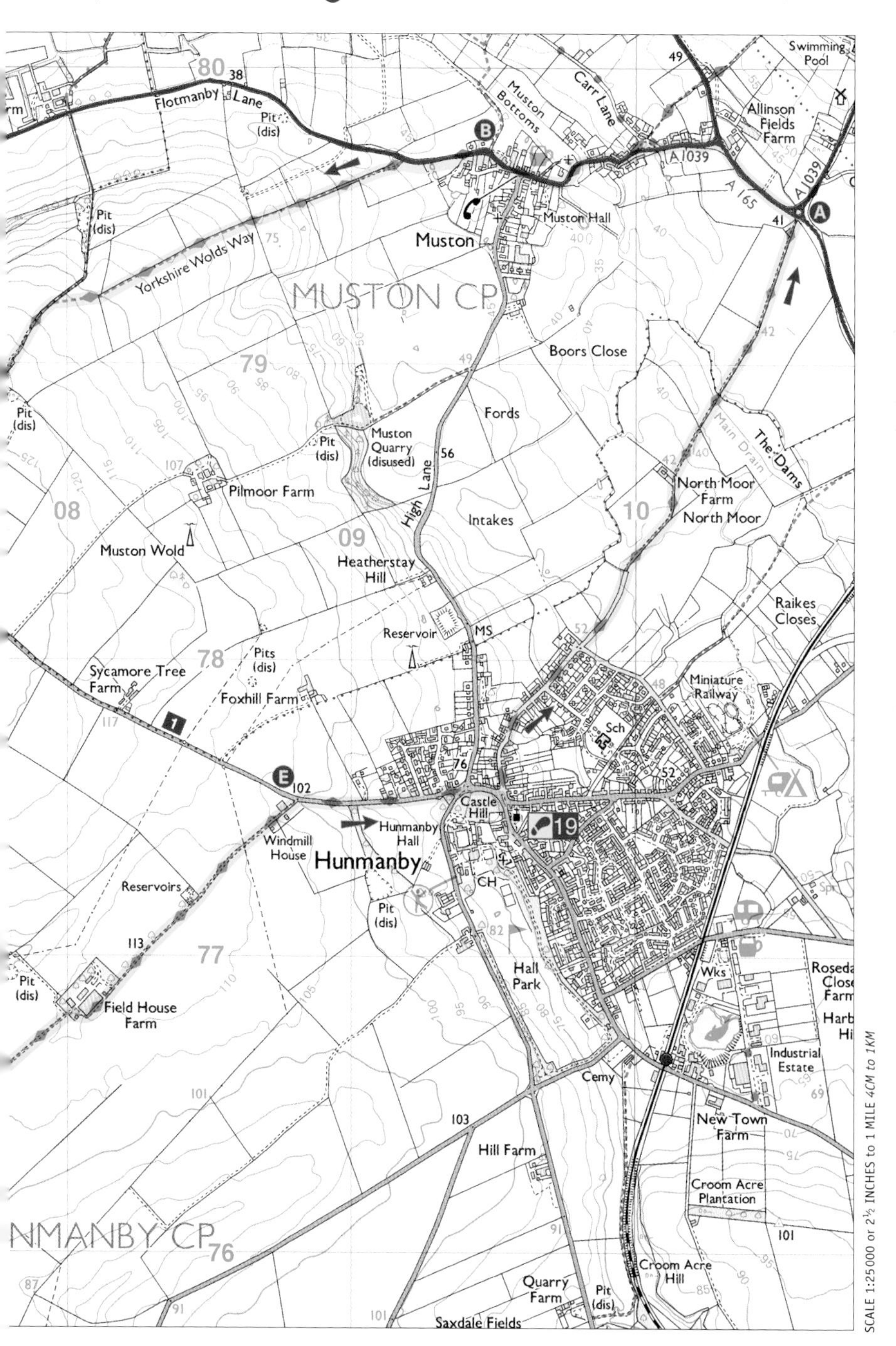

Londesborough Park and Goodmanham

Start	Market Weighton
Distance	7¾ miles (12.5km)
Height gain	410 feet (125m)
Approximate time	3¾ hours
Parking	Market Weighton
Ordnance Survey maps	Landranger 106 (Market Weighton), Explorer 294 (Market Weighton & Yorkshire Wolds Central)

GPS waypoints

- Start SE 877 417
- A SE 871 421
- B SE 869 446
- C SE 870 453
- D SE 868 453
- E SE 878 440
- F SE 890 431
- G SE 899 426

Almost the whole of this ramble is on the Yorkshire Wolds Way, using alternative routes between Market Weighton and Londesborough Park which afford extensive views over the wolds and the Vale of York. The stretch through Londesborough Park is particularly pleasant, continuing across country to the attractive village of Goodmanham. A descent into Spring Dale is followed by a final leg along a disused railway.

Market Weighton's traditional importance as a focus of transport was enhanced by the arrival of a canal in the 18th century and then the railway 100 years later. Both have since gone but the old railway line to Beverley now serves as a public footpath and is followed during the last part of the route. Probably the town's most famous son was William Bradley, the Yorkshire Giant, born in 1787. He grew to a height of 7 feet 9 inches (2.36m) and weighed 27 stone (172kg).

From Market Place facing the **Londesborough Arms**, a fine example of a Georgian coaching inn, walk along the main street left past the church, which lies behind the buildings on the right. Keep with it as it bends to become York Road. Reaching the edge of town, leave through a kissing-gate on the right **A**. Signed the Wilberforce and Yorkshire Wolds Way, a path strikes across the crop, following a line of power-cable posts. Over a bridged ditch, continue at the edge of more fields until you hit a main road, Towthorpe Lane.

An avenued track opposite leads on to Towthorpe Grange. Walk past the farm and barn to a gate into the field beyond. A trod guides you across pasture to a gap in the far belt of trees. Cross Towthorpe Beck and bear right across the next field. Continue by the brook at the edge of subsequent fields until you reach a lane **B**.

Go left, but after 75 yds, turn through the lodge gates into Londesborough Park. Still following Wilberforce and Yorkshire Wolds Way signs, pass through a kissing-gate and continue on a grass track, which later rises to a signposted fork Ⓒ.

The left branch is signed to Londesborough and climbs towards a wood. Walk through the trees to emerge at the edge of the village and turn left to the church Ⓓ.

During its history the Londesborough estate has had a succession of owners, including the earls of Burlington, the Cavendish family (dukes of Devonshire), George Hudson, the 19th-century 'Railway King', and the earls of Londesborough. It was the third Earl of Burlington who landscaped the park, including the lake. The Cavendishes largely neglected it in favour of their main residence at Chatsworth, and the old hall was demolished in 1819. A new one was built in 1839, but on a different site. The earls of Londesborough, who owned the estate from 1850 to 1923, enlarged the new house and restored the parkland. The modest but attractive church has a Saxon sun dial and fine Norman south door, the porch being added in 1679.

Retrace your steps to Ⓒ and now go left, the path descending to cross a stream. Where the rising track beyond forks, bear right, cutting across the park to a kissing-gate. Cross a bridge above a weir forming one of the many lakes at the head of Towthorpe Beck. Carry on across the field beyond, a trod guiding you past the corner of Pond Wood to a kissing-gate at the top of the park. Joining a gravel track, follow it right, but where it later veers away, keep ahead at the field margin, a sign guiding you towards Goodmanham.

Meeting the main road Ⓔ, carefully cross to the entrance of the Towthorpe Corner picnic site, but where the lane almost immediately bends right, bear off left to pick up a descending field track, signed the Yorkshire Wolds Way. Swinging left at the corner, the way continues at the perimeter of successive fields, eventually curving right to pass beneath the bridge of a disused railway. Rising beyond to a fork, take the left

Goodmanham church

branch up into Goodmanham and follow the ensuing street ahead to a junction by the church F.

With traces of settlement back to the Stone Age, there are claims that the village is one of the earliest religious sites in the country. All Hallows Church is reputed to stand on the site of a pagan temple dedicated to the Anglo-Saxon god Woden. Christianity spread here during the 7th century and, following King Edwin's conversion after hearing Paulinus preach at nearby Londesborough, he sacked the temple in establishing the new faith in his land.

You'll find the **Goodmanham Arms** just to the right, but the onward way is up to the left. Reaching the outskirts of the village, turn off right along a narrow lane, undulating between herb-rich banks into Spring Dale. Over to the right there are glimpses to Market Weighton, its square-towered church distinguished from the other buildings. After almost 3/4 mile (1.2km), as the lane twists through an S-bend, leave through a gap on the right onto the Hudson Way G, an almost dead-straight path pursuing the course of a former railway towards Market Weighton. Opened in 1865 and operational for 100 years, the line connected the town to Beverley, while that passed earlier, to the north of Goodmanham ran via Great Driffield to the coast.

Approaching the town, the way opens out. Keep the left branch, which runs onto the end of a street. Bear left on a path at the edge of grass, going left again along a short track to reach another street. Walk to the end and go left and then right, passing around the church to return to Market Place. ●

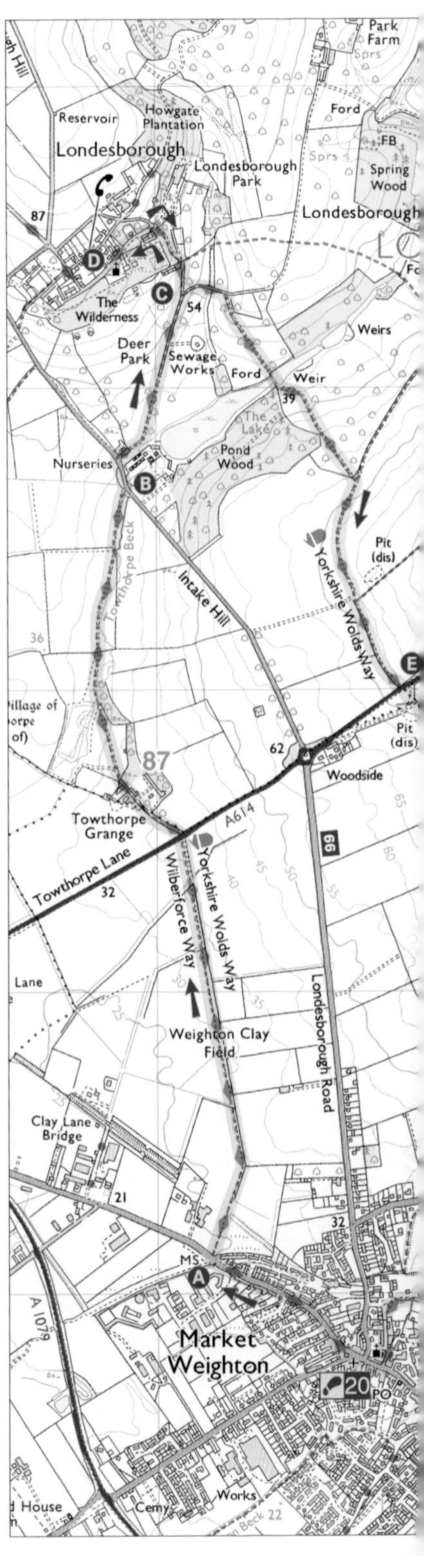

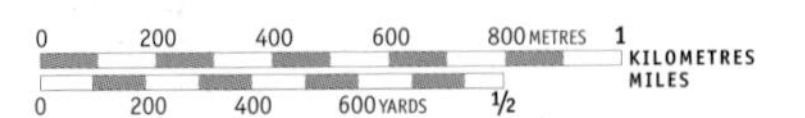

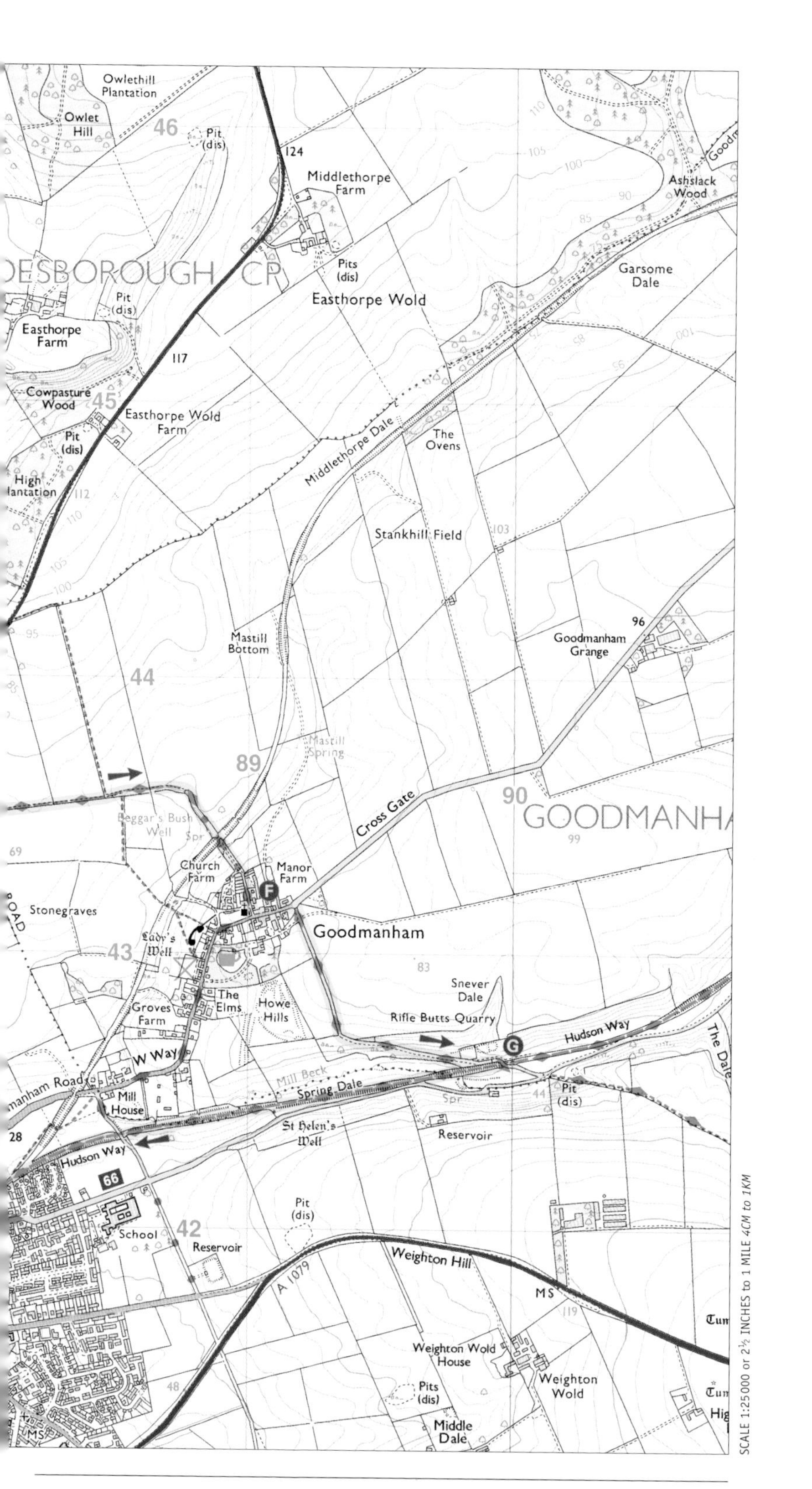

SCALE 1:25 000 or 2½ INCHES to 1 MILE *4CM to 1KM*

Cowlam and Cottam

Start	Cowlam Manor
Distance	8 miles (12.9km)
Height gain	740 feet (225m)
Approximate time	4 hours
Parking	Rough verge on western side of lane near entrance to Cowlam Manor (do not block field or farm access), 2 miles (3.2km) east of Sledmere
Ordnance Survey maps	Landranger 101 (Scarborough, Bridlington & Filey), Explorer 300 (Howardian Hills & Malton)

GPS waypoints

Start	SE 965 654
A	SE 975 648
B	SE 972 634
C	SE 996 639
D	SE 994 648
E	SE 988 656
F	SE 978 659

The deep, secretive folds of the Yorkshire Wolds are contrasted by far-reaching vistas from the rolling hilltops that enclose them. A couple of abandoned medieval villages, each with a church, a Roman road and remnants of a wartime airfield all add interest to this exhilarating walk.

The medieval village site at Cottam is one of the best preserved in the county, its many humps and bumps clearly marking building platforms and a hollow lane. Also obvious are cultivation terraces above the dale head. The church is Victorian, but now disused, has become derelict. Nearby, the concrete structures were an air-raid shelter. The hilltop was intended as a wartime bomber base, but the unpredictability of winds funnelled by

A frosty spring morning in Cowlam Well Dale

Cottam church and medieval village

the surrounding dales rendered it dangerous and it functioned largely as a bomb and munitions store.

Turn into Church Farm, walking past the farmhouse and ahead through the yard beyond. Fork right in front of a gate and then at the next fork, keep right again, passing through a gate into the narrow, deepening fold of Cowlam Well Dale. Towards the bottom, beyond the fenced enclosure of a dew pond, bear right through a bridle gate A and continue along Phillip's Slack. Reaching Cottam Well Dale, go ahead through a bridle gate and turn right beside the hedge. Carry on for over 3/4 mile (1.2km), passing the foot of the short stub of Elvin Lear and eventually emerging through a bridle gate on the right onto a lane B.

Walk left for nearly 1/2 mile (800m) before leaving opposite a track through a small, signposted gate on the left. The bridleway steadily climbs away, the path initially hedged before opening to a wider track from which there are superb views across Garton Bottom to the foot of Warren Dale. Beyond a dip at the head of Lambert Dale, the way rises steadily onward, abruptly becoming concreted (part of the old airbase) towards the crest of the hill.

Reaching a junction C, turn off left towards farm buildings, erected on what was the main runway. Where the track later swings sharply right, leave left on a green track towards woodland surrounding Cottam House.

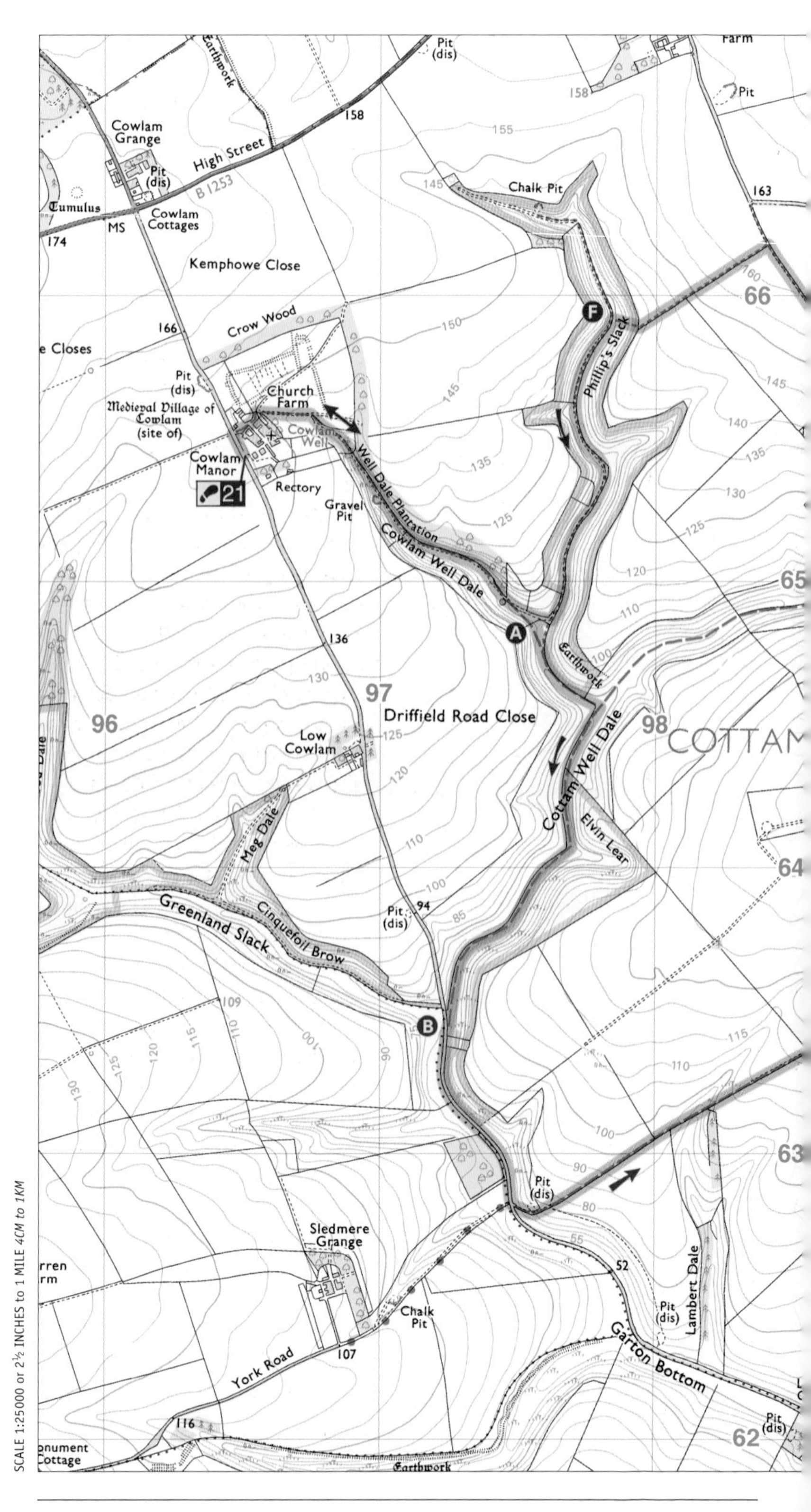

SCALE 1:25000 or 2½ INCHES to 1 MILE 4CM to 1KM

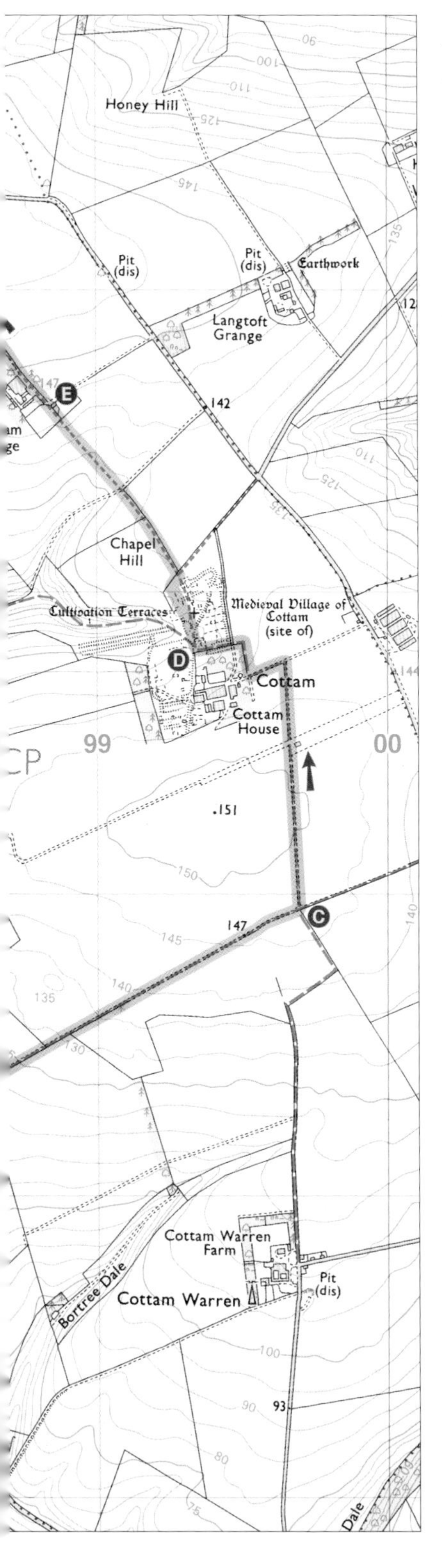

Approaching the trees, swing right, going left at the corner to meet a metalled farm track **D**. Cross to a gate opposite and bear slightly right, dropping towards a second gate, a place from which to take in the extensive earthworks outlining the abandoned village.

The way lies to the right, passing below the crumbling ruin of Cottam Holy Trinity Church. Approaching a fence, wind right to a kissing-gate. Walk away by the right boundary towards a white house, passing through more gates before ultimately emerging on a drive beside the Foreman's House at Cottam Grange **E**. Go left through a large yard to leave along its access track.

Towards its end, leave through a gap in the fence on the left to join a field-edge gravel track downhill. Where that later swings left, continue down on grass to a gate at the bottom corner. Head steeply down beside a fence into Phillip's Slack, crossing a stile at the bottom **F**. Follow the dale gently down for 3/4 mile (1.2km) to return to the foot of Cowlam Well Dale. Turn through a gate there **A** and head back up the dale to Church Farm at Cowlam.

There was a medieval village here too, sited to the north of Church Farm, but it is less obvious than that at Cottam with its outlines largely lost. However, the little church, which dates back to the 10th century, is still in use and well worth a look. Inside is a lovely example of an early carved font, depicting images of, among others, Adam and Eve, Jacob and Esau and the three magi visiting Jesus. It is accessed from the lane just to the south via the entrance to the adjacent Cowlam Manor Farm.

0 200 400 600 800 METRES 1 KILOMETRES
MILES
0 200 400 600 YARDS 1/2

Tadcaster and Healaugh

Start	Tadcaster, at north end of the bridge over the River Wharfe
Distance	8¼ miles (13.3km)
Height gain	180 feet (55m)
Approximate time	4 hours
Parking	Tadcaster
Ordnance Survey maps	Landranger 105 (York & Selby), Explorer 290 (York)

GPS waypoints

- Start: SE 487 435
- A: SE 485 435
- B: SE 480 435
- C: SE 486 439
- D: SE 489 446
- E: SE 496 478
- F: SE 500 475
- G: SE 493 448

After a short opening stretch beside the Wharfe to the church, the route winds through the outskirts of town to an impressive viaduct across the river. Taking to the fields, the way follows an old track past the site of a medieval monastery to the neighbouring village of Healaugh, distinguished by its fine Norman church. The return is by way of field paths across a gently undulating countryside.

Tadcaster is famous for its breweries and, when the wind is right, the tantalising aroma from the mash drifts over the opening and closing stages of the walk. The earliest records of brewing in the town go back to the 14th century, when it would have been largely a cottage industry supplying domestic needs, but by the 17th century it had become very much a big business and a succession of companies were established. The Old Brewery was opened in 1758 and is Yorkshire's oldest. Samuel Smith's still take water from the original well and use stone 'squares', traditional solid slate brewing vessels to ferment the wort. And come on the right day and you may see shire horses pulling the dray stacked with barrels to make deliveries around the town. Tadcaster's two other surviving breweries are John Smith's, now part of the Scottish Courage group and the Tower Brewery, owned by Coors and passed near the start of the ramble. The reason for such a concentration of brewing in the town was the pure, hard water that seeps up through the bedrock in 'popple' wells, as this enabled the production of a very clear, bitter beer.

Start in Commercial Street at the northern end of the town's 18th-century bridge spanning the River Wharfe. Cross, but then immediately leave along a riverside path signed right to the Viaduct and Newton Kyme. Turn off just beyond the church **A** on a path skirting around the churchyard and past a row of houses to emerge on a street. The first stone church on the site was built in the 12th century and was held by Sawley Abbey on the River Ribble, far to the west. Rebuilt in the 14th century after destruction by the Scots, the church was frequently

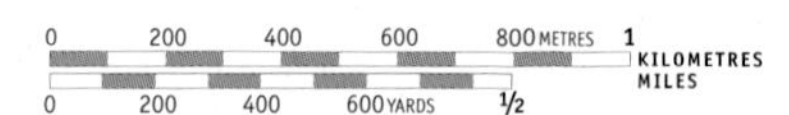

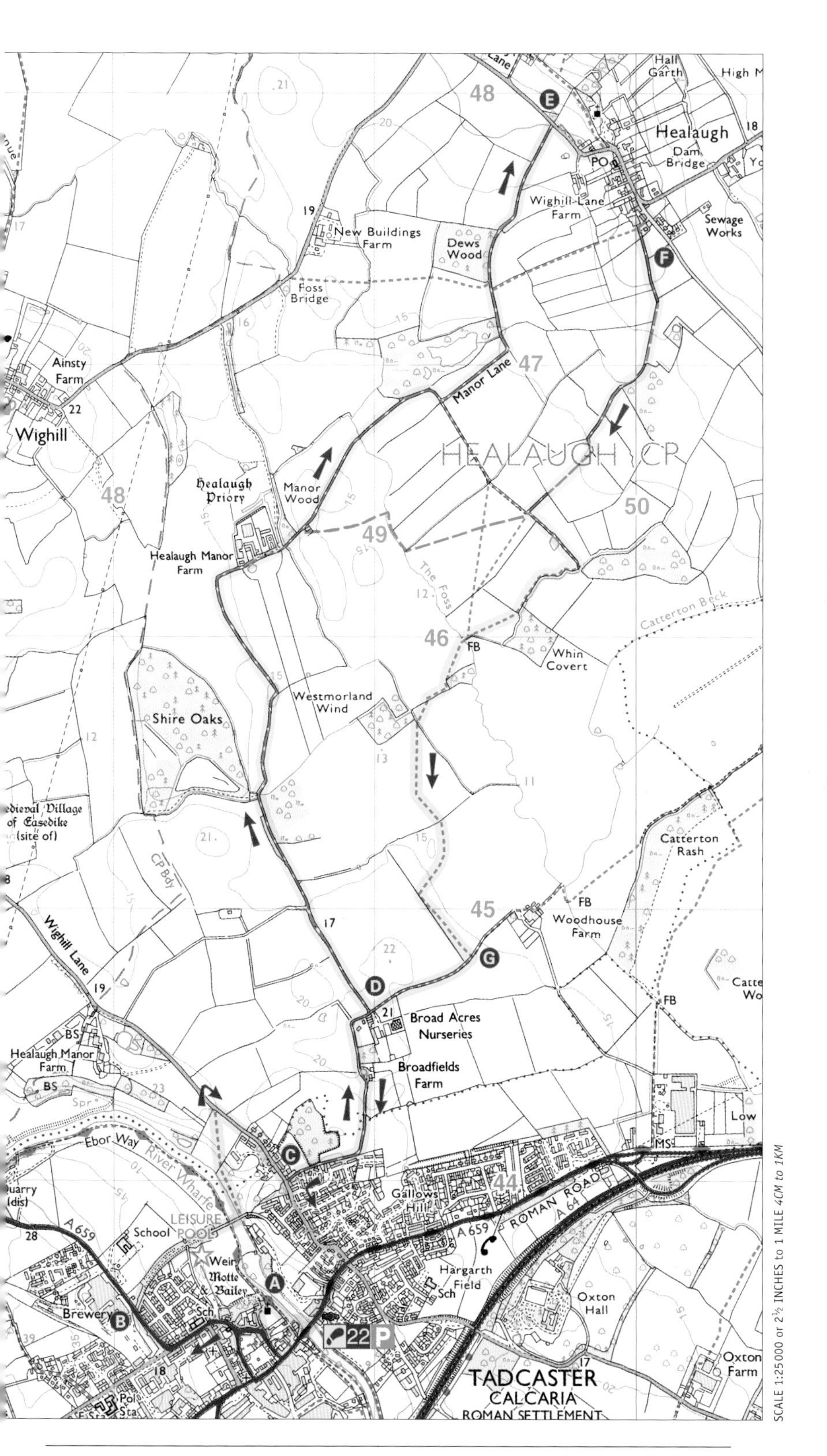

SCALE 1:25 000 or 2½ INCHES to 1 MILE *4CM to 1KM*

Tadcaster church

flooded and in 1857 it was dismantled and rebuilt upon raised foundations. Go sharp right along Westgate and fork right past the war memorial, walking on to reach the second road leaving on the right. Signed to Boston Spa and Wetherby, it leads past the Coors Tower Brewery, opposite which a footpath is signed off as the Viaduct Walk **B**.

Built in 1849 by the railway magnate, George Hudson, the viaduct remained a white elephant for 30 years for his financial empire collapsed before the railway itself was built. It was later used to service a mill on the eastern bank of the Wharfe, but that finished in 1955 and it now serves as an impressive footbridge.

On the far bank, drop right, pass beneath the bridge and continue on a path through rough ground beside the river. Approaching a fence bear right up to a waymarked stile and strike a diagonal line across the pasture beyond to meet the road at its far top corner. Go right for some 300 yds to a signed bridleway along a track to the left **C**. Follow it for 1/2 mile (800m) past Broadfields Farm to a junction **D**.

Go left, ignoring a later turning and eventually winding around to Healaugh Manor Farm, built on the site of a former 13th-century Augustinian priory. Walk ahead past the buildings and keep on through a barrier, ultimately reaching a junction of tracks. Swing left with the main track, finally coming out onto a lane **E**.

To the right, the lane winds into the village, passing below the church, set back above the road, which has a splendidly decorated Norman doorway. At the other end of the village, where the lane bends left, keep ahead on a narrower lane signed to Catterton. Take the second turning off on the right, after 100 yds into Town End Farm **F**.

Walk through to leave at the far-left corner along a winding track. Keep ahead through a couple of gates part way along. Entering a field at the end, carry on to a gate at the far side. A short track leads through another gate to a T-junction – here turn left. Just before it finishes, turn through a gate on the right and follow the left hedge. Cross a double stile by the edge of a wood and strike a diagonal across the next field.

Over a stile and footbridge, bear left across the field corner towards trees and continue along the left-hand boundary. After 200 yds at a waymark, angle left through the broken hedge and strike across the corner of the adjacent field to a prominent waypost. Pass into the next field and head away on a left diagonal, maintaining the same course in the field beyond that along a line set by three oaks. Reaching the far boundary, follow the hedge left to emerge onto a track **G**.

To the right, it leads back before too long to the junction **D** encountered on the outward journey. Keep ahead to retrace your steps to the road **C**, but now turn left. Reaching traffic lights at the end, go right and walk downhill back to Tadcaster Bridge.

October 2020.

Hornsea Mere and the Rail Trail

Start	Hornsea, corner of Marine Drive and New Road
Distance	8½ miles (13.7km)
Height gain	Negligible
Approximate time	4 hours
Parking	Hornsea
Ordnance Survey maps	Landranger 107 (Kingston upon Hull), Explorer 295 (Bridlington, Driffield & Hornsea)

GPS waypoints

- Start: TA 208 481
- A: TA 200 475
- B: TA 198 466
- C: TA 168 466
- D: TA 166 450
- E: TA 171 448
- F: TA 188 445

Leaving the town, this longer but undemanding walk passes Yorkshire's largest natural lake, Hornsea Mere. After skirting Wassand Park, it returns along country lanes to follow the eastern end of the Trans Pennine Trail back to the coast.

Leave the seafront at the southern end of Marine Drive, walking inland along New Road. Keep ahead through the shopping area as it becomes Newbegin, to traffic lights by St Nicholas' Church **A**. Go left along Southgate, following it for a over ¼ mile (400m) before turning off into Hull Road.

Head away through the residential outskirts, soon getting your first glimpse of Hornsea Mere to the right. After nearly ½ mile (800m) and just before reaching the town's boundary, leave through a kissing-gate on the right into a large meadow bordering the lake **B**.

Barely a mile (1.6km) from the sea, the mere is a feature from the last ice age and, although over two miles (3.2km) long, is only 12 feet (3.7m) at its deepest. Extensive reed beds line the shores, which attract several uncommon species of insects and moths and many varieties of ducks and geese are to be seen on the waters throughout the year. The mere is also a noted breeding site for reed warblers.

Strike half left on a trod to a kissing-gate, continuing at the left side of a second meadow. Beyond another kissing-gate carry on at the edge of successive crop fields, eventually passing through a kissing-gate onto open pasture once more. Bearing left of centre, cross to a gate at the far side and maintain

Hornsea Rail Trail

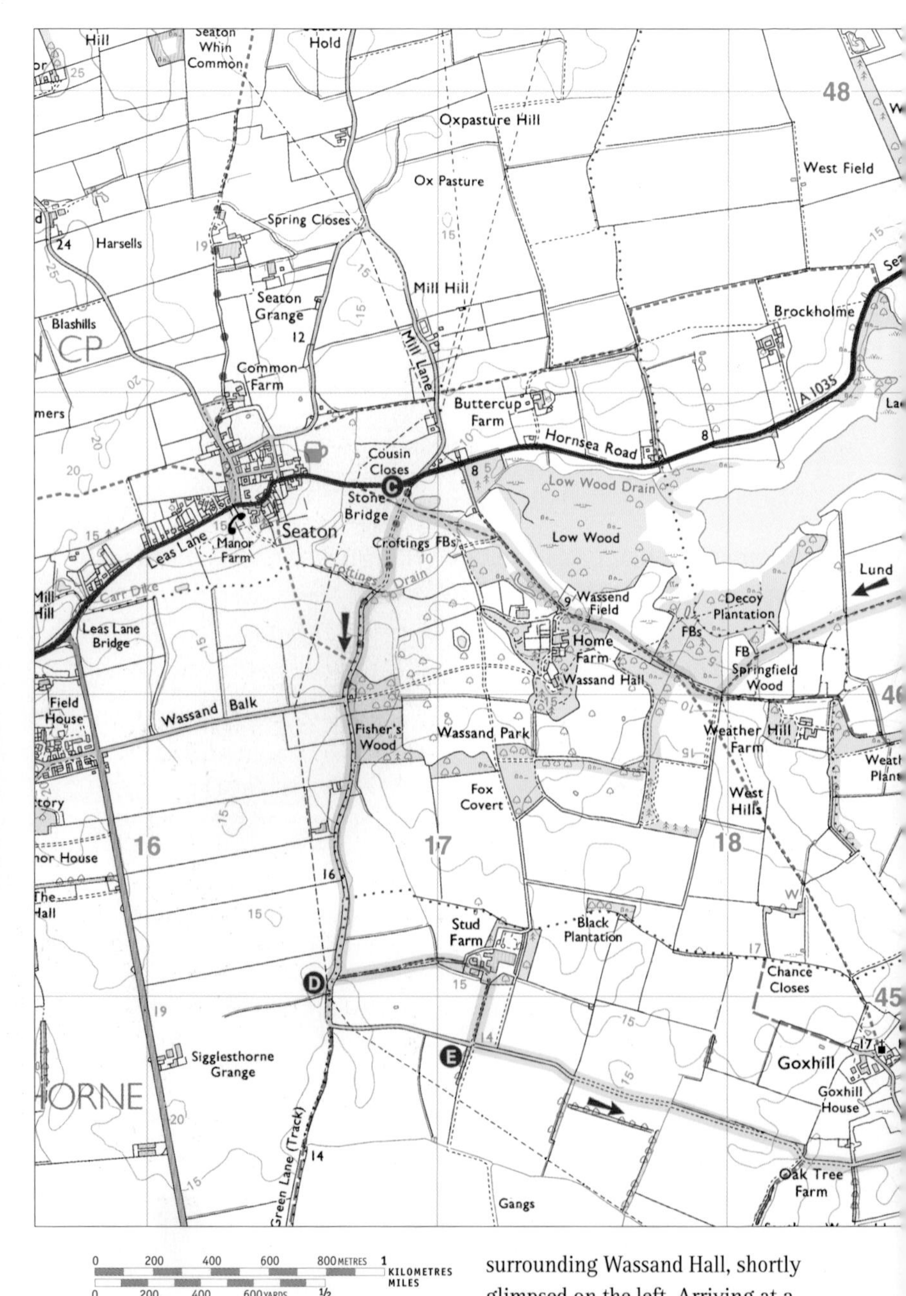

your line across the field beyond. Over a gated bridge, continue on the same diagonal heading in a final field. Exit from the far right corner onto a track.

Through a gate to the right, it winds gently through wooded parkland surrounding Wassand Hall, shortly glimpsed on the left. Arriving at a junction by Home Farm, bear right along the main drive. After some 400 yds, at a waymark hidden in trees, take the track on the left, but then immediately bear off right along a path through a small larch plantation. Pass beyond the trees to emerge through a

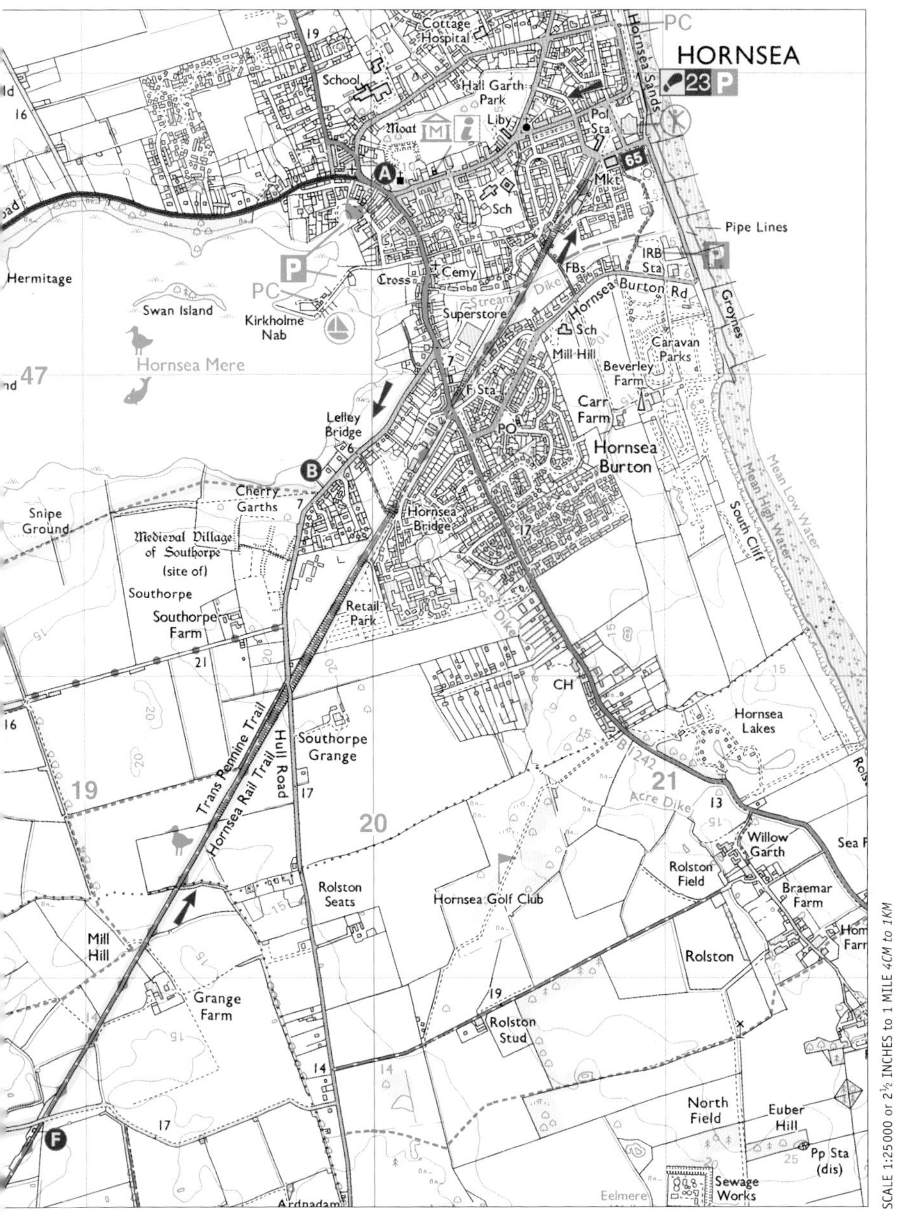

kissing-gate into rough pasture. Walk on, paralleling a fence to intercept a grass track **C**.

Turn left, going through a gate at the top of the field to continue within the fringe of a belt of trees. The track ends at the corner of a lane by an estate lodge. Walk ahead for some ½ mile (800m) and then look for a gate and footpath signpost concealed in the left hedge, just before overhead pylon cables close with the lane **D**.

Follow the field edge away to a gate in the corner and carry on along a fenced track towards Stud Farm. Just before a sharp left bend, slip through a waymarked bridle-gate on the right and go left to a field gate. Walk forward on grass past the farmhouse to a yard. Pass through, leaving to the right along its access drive to return to the lane E.

Turn left and walk for a mile (1.6km), continuing over a crossroads. A little farther on, just after a cottage, leave along a path off left signed 'Hornsea Rail Trail' F.

It follows the trackbed of the former Hull – Hornsea Railway, which opened in 1864 and operated for 100 years before closure under Beeching. The way runs straight for over 1¼ miles (2km), passing beneath a road bridge and later abruptly ending by houses. Go right to reach a street and follow it left to a roundabout junction. Cross to a footpath directly opposite, which resumes the course of the railway atop a wooded embankment into the town. It ends beside the old station building. Turn right towards the seafront and then go left along the promenade past the leisure centre back to the start.

Hornsea Mere

Stamford Bridge

Start	Stamford Bridge
Distance	8¾ miles (13.9km)
Height gain	Negligible
Approximate time	4 hours
Parking	Riverside car park at Stamford Bridge
Ordnance Survey maps	Landranger 105 (York & Selby) or 106 (Market Weighton, Goole and Stamford Bridge), Explorers 290 (York) and 294 (Market Weighton & Yorkshire Wolds Central)

GPS waypoints

- SE 711 555
- Ⓐ SE 712 552
- Ⓑ SE 699 554
- Ⓒ SE 694 521
- Ⓓ SE 703 510

This fine walk is a lengthy but easy-going exploration of the Derwent valley south of Stamford Bridge, site of the last great Viking battle on British soil and prequel to William of Normandy's invasion in 1066.

Stamford Bridge saw the last great battle against Viking invaders on English soil in 1066. After a forced march from the south, bolstering his army along the way, King Harold defeated the Norwegian Harald Hardrada, who had his eye on the throne and had teamed up with Harold's brother Tostig Godwinson, who had his own gripe with the king. Harold managed to catch the invading force off guard, but it was nevertheless a bloody affair, with some 11,000 men killed on the battlefield, including Harald and Tostig. But Harold's triumph was short lived, for only four days later, William of Normandy landed at Pevensey Bay on the Channel coast. Harold immediately headed back south, marching with heavy armour more than 250 miles in a fortnight to confront the new interloper at Hastings. The day was hard fought, and had Harold not been killed late in the day, history might have been different. But with their leader gone, the exhausted army fell apart and William went on to claim the English crown.

Leaving the car park, turn right along Viking Road. Keeping out of cul de sacs, follow its winding course through a small residential estate. At the top, go right along Church Road, walking as far as the former Stamford Bridge railway station, marked by a single level crossing gatel Ⓐ.

Turn right between the platforms, still complete with the waiting rooms and small transit warehouse, to continue on a shared pedestrian/cycle track following the old rail bed. A long viaduct and bridge takes it over the River Derwent before emerging onto the main road. The route follows the pavement to the left past a drive before tucking into a belt of conifers beside the road. Emerging at the far end, leave the main road at the first turning Ⓑ, a narrow private lane signed as a cycleway to Dunnington.

The way runs as a tree-lined drive to Hendwick Hall, winding on beyond. Later on, keep ahead past a junction to

Stamford Bridge station

Lime Field Farm, passing Scoreby Manor House and eventually reaching a junction where a track leaves to Londesborough Lodge Farm **C**.

However, go left and then swing right, walking a little further to a point where the main track swings right. Leave left at that point on a gravel track signed to Kexby.

After passing through Millfield Wood, the track narrows to a path. Watch for it then swinging right through the hedge to continue as an unbounded path between the fields. Towards the far end, it broadens to a track, which leads out to the main road beside a large care home, Derwent House **D**. Turn left and follow the main road a short distance to a bridge across the River Derwent. The old bridge still stands just downstream and can be seen from the main road, but you can take a closer look by turning right onto the old road opposite the care home.

Returning to the main road, head towards the new bridge, but leave left behind the crash barrier immediately before it onto a path heading upstream above the river. The way soon falls to continue along the pleasantly tree-lined river bank, crossing stiled footbridges over occasional side streams and through gates from field to field. In time, there is a glimpse of Low Catton on the opposite bank, but unfortunately there is no bridge across the river to the pub there. A little further on, eagle eyes might spot the viaduct over which you began the walk.

Eventually, after 3¼ miles (5.25km) beside the river, the way leads beneath the high bridge and viaduct, a much more impressive structure when seen from below. The path then shortly meets the road bridge, climbing out there to

0 200 400 600 800 METRES 1 KILOMETRES
0 200 400 600 YARDS ½ MILES

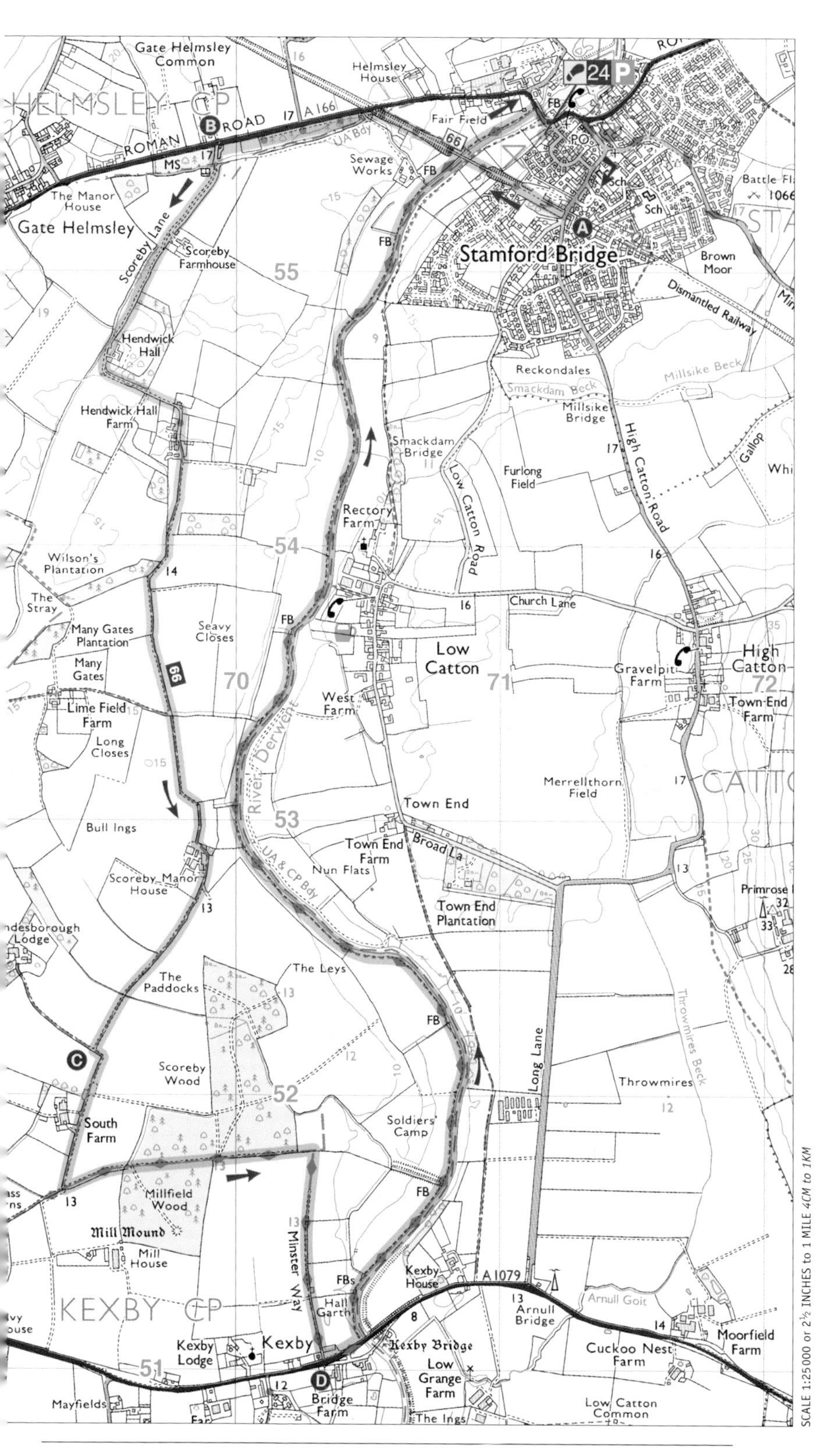

SCALE 1:25000 or 2½ INCHES to 1 MILE *4CM to 1KM*

the pavement. However, you might first wander on beside the tail of the old mill stream up to a sluice gate. The land to the right is a small island on which stood a corn mill. The present complex is thought to date from the end of the 17th century, although earlier mills occupied the same site. It was significantly extended in the 19th century, with two waterwheels powering seven pairs of millstones. It continued in use until 1964 and has since been converted into private apartments.

Return to the south side of the bridge to rejoin the road, crossing to take advantage of the pedestrian bridge just upstream. On the far side, re-cross the main road back to Viking Road and the car park.

Stamford's railway bridge and viaduct across the River Derwent

Nether Poppleton and the River Ouse

Start	Nether Poppleton
Distance	9 miles (14.5km)
Height gain	Negligible
Approximate time	4 hours
Parking	Parking by the church at Nether Poppleton
Ordnance Survey maps	Landranger 105 (York & Selby), Explorer 290 (York)

GPS waypoints

- SE 564 550
- Ⓐ SE 556 549
- Ⓑ SE 540 553
- Ⓒ SE 516 561
- Ⓓ SE 512 569
- Ⓔ SE 512 578

The first half of this lengthy, although easy walk in the flat countryside that lies to the west of York meanders across fields to the banks of the River Nidd near Moor Monkton. After following the Nidd to its confluence with the Ouse, the return wanders through a succession of riverbank meadows. The walk begins from the small Norman church in Nether Poppleton, which has a picturesque setting beside a restored tithe barn and village pond.

The delightful 12th-century church is one of only two in the country dedicated to St Everilda, a little-known Saxon lady. She is said to have founded a humble monastery at Everingham, where there was also a holy well dedicated to her. The tithe barn, recently restored, dates from the early 16th century, although the brickwork was added about 200 years later.

From the church, follow the track back past the tithe barn. Leave just past the duck pond through a kissing-gate on the left. Signed at the edge of a paddock to Millfield Lane, the path affords a fine view along the valley to the distant towers of York Minster. Meeting a street, the way continues between the houses opposite to emerge on Millfield Lane. Go right and then swing left past a junction with Church Lane to carry on through the village. After 1/4 mile (400m), just beyond Riverside Gardens, leave over a stile on the right Ⓐ.

Stride along a path at the edge of successive fields, the way swapping to the left flank of the hedge as you approach New Farm. Emerging from the field, briefly follow a track towards the farm, but abandon it after a few yards through a gate on the right. Go left on a gravel track past the buildings, but where it then turns left beyond the corner of a barn, move right to enter a field. Carry on beside a ditch on your left, curving within a shallow corner and, through a hedge gap, continue at the edge of the next field to meet a track, Lords Lane Ⓑ.

To the right it heads to Woodhouse Farm. Approaching the converted barn, look for a footpath off left at the corner of a wooden fence. Signed to Moor Monkton, it leads to a small pasture.

Over the stile, strike left to another stile beside a gate at the far side. Cross The Foss and continue along another field to reach a track by the next farm. Turn right, not along the track, but through the field gate just beyond it and walk away with the hedge on your right around two sides of the field. Leave through a gate and follow a tarmac drive past the front of the large house at Thickpenny Farm.

Just beyond it, bear off right through a wooden gate and follow a gravel track on past a cottage, which ultimately leads out to a narrow lane. Through a gate opposite, head across grazing to a wood at the far side and turn left along its edge. Passing through a gate, carry on beside a deep ditch. Keep with the ditch when it shortly swings right, following it to a gate **C**.

A hedge-lined path leads on to the next field, the route continuing at the

0 200 400 600 800 METRES 1 KILOMETRES
MILES
0 200 400 600 YARDS ½

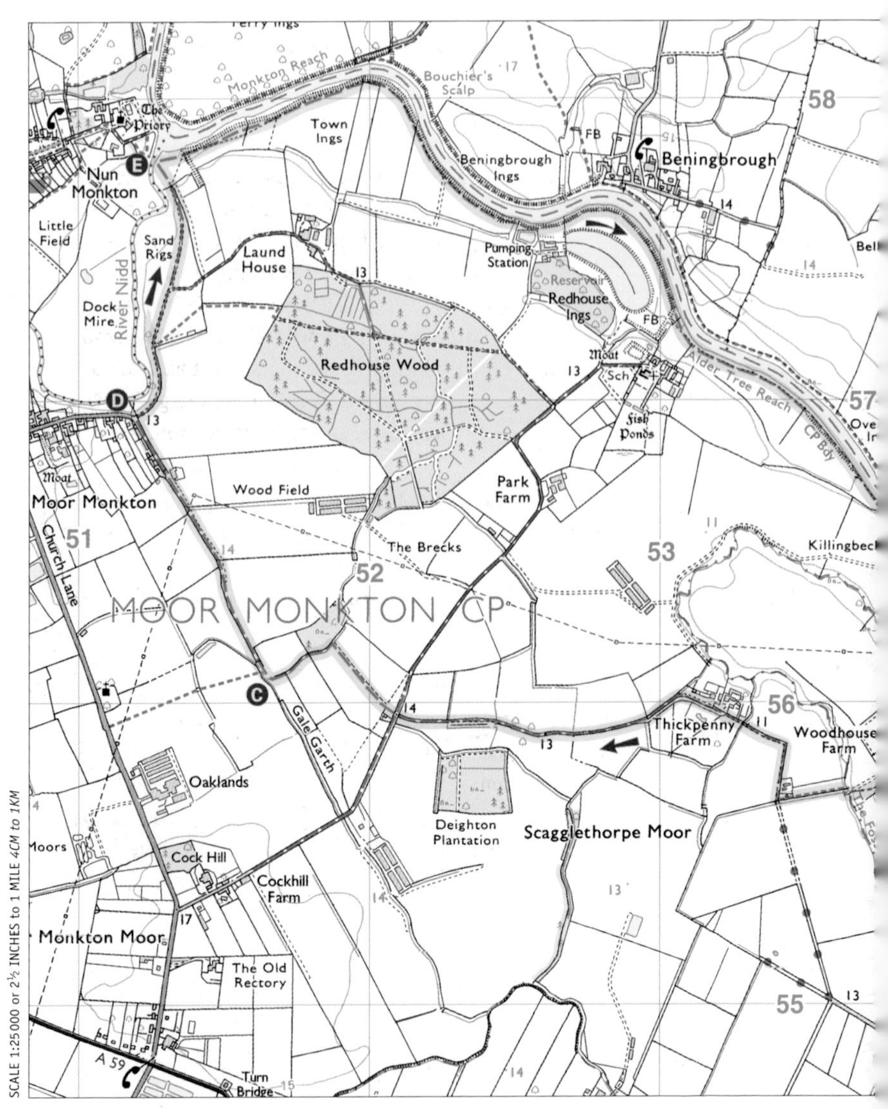

SCALE 1:25000 or 2½ INCHES to 1 MILE *4CM to 1KM*

perimeter of successive fields before finally emerging onto the end of a track. Running past a row of cottages, it develops as a lane. As it subsequently bends left towards the village of Moor Monkton, turn off right on a track to Laund House Farm **D**.

Where the track later swings right, signed to Redhouse Wood, keep ahead on a grass track above the River Nidd. Towards the far end, bear left down the bank to pass through a double gate. Walk across open grazing to a waypost beside the confluence of the rivers Nidd and Ouse **E**, from where there is a fine view across the water to the houses and church of Nun Monkton. It is the site of a 12th-century Benedictine nunnery founded by William de Arches for his daughter Maud, who served as its first prioress.

Follow the riverbank downstream, ambling at the edge of successive pastures, now protected from flooding by a raised embankment. The lake shortly passed is a reservoir storing water, which is pumped from the river.

River Ouse near Nether Poppleton

Later on, passing Killingbecks, the path briefly diverges from the bank before delving back through an unkempt corner to a bridge spanning a small side stream. Eventually passing through a gate as you approach Nether Poppleton, the pathway becomes surfaced. As it then swings right, bear off across a bridge to meet the lane. Follow it left back to the village, this time turning along Church Lane to return to the start point.

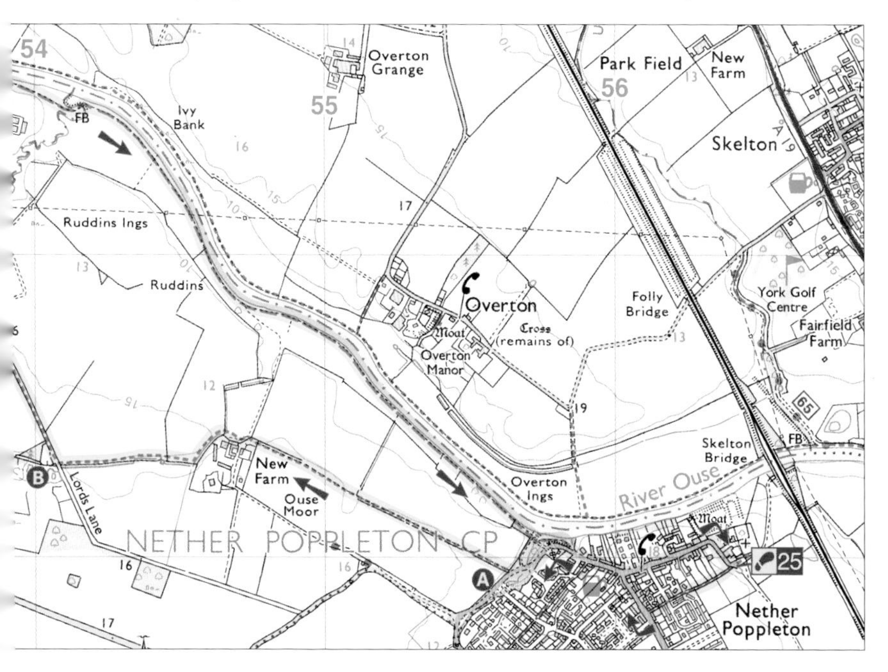

Welton Dale and Brantingham Wold

Start	Welton
Distance	8¾ miles (14.2km)
Height gain	965 feet (295m)
Approximate time	4½ hours
Parking	Some parking spaces around the Green at Welton in front of the Green Dragon
Ordnance Survey maps	Landranger 106 (Market Weighton), Explorer 293 (Kingston upon Hull & Beverley)

GPS waypoints

- SE 957 272
- Ⓐ SE 967 292
- Ⓑ SE 963 288
- Ⓒ SE 947 298
- Ⓓ SE 943 300
- Ⓔ SE 972 304
- Ⓕ SE 966 279

This pleasing walk on the southern edge of the Yorkshire Wolds takes you through a classic wolds landscape of attractive villages nestling within narrow wooded valleys below rolling, unbounded uplands. From the higher and more open parts of the route, the views extend across the wolds to the Vale of York, the River Humber and Hull.

Welton has all the ingredients of a traditional English village, with old cottages, duck pond, welcoming pub and ancient church gathered around a picturesque green and it claims fame in that Dick Turpin's life of crime finally came to an end at the Green Dragon. Posing outward respectability under the guise of John Palmer, Turpin had taken up as a horse dealer, but during a drunken spree he shot the landlord's cockerel and ended up in gaol. As enquiries began to reveal his sordid past, he wrote to his brother-in-law in Essex for help. But he refused to pay the 6d postage and the letter reverted to the postmaster who recognised Turpin's handwriting. His identity exposed, Turpin was tried for horse stealing and subsequently hanged at York on April 7, 1793.

Leave the **Green Dragon** along Cowgate, walking past the pond and church to a junction. Keep ahead along Dale Road, which shortly degrades to a track into the Welton Dale Estate. Reaching Dale Cottage, bear right past it to a gate. The path continues between woodland and meadow into the solitude of the upper valley. The way later passes back into trees before meeting a concrete track Ⓐ.

Cross to a kissing-gate opposite, through which follow the field edge left to emerge at the top onto a lane. Head downhill for 1/4 mile (400m) before abandoning it in favour of a footpath leaving through a gate into the wood on the right Ⓑ. Eventually reaching a crossing of paths, take the one ahead signed to Brantingham. Wind down amongst the trees, swinging right past a junction to come out onto another lane. Through a kissing-gate opposite,

0 200 400 600 800 METRES 1 KILOMETRES
MILES
0 200 400 600 YARDS 1/2

continue with the ongoing path, which before long climbs to a junction. Go right, but when you reach a metal gate, swing left through a gap and follow the path until you eventually meet another lane **C**.

For refreshment head downhill into Brantingham. At the bottom, keep left to find the post office and **The Triton Inn** at the other end of the village. The church, however, lies to the right along Dale Road, which although locked stands in a beautiful setting **D**.

From the lychgate, retrace your steps along the track in front of Church Cottage, leaving through a kissing-gate on the left, just before it merges with the lane. A contained path, signed the Yorkshire Wolds Way heads upfield to the top lane, which you should follow back up to **C**.

Now carry on uphill, keeping ahead along a hedged, gravel track where the lane turns into Wold View Farm over Brantingham Wold. Reaching

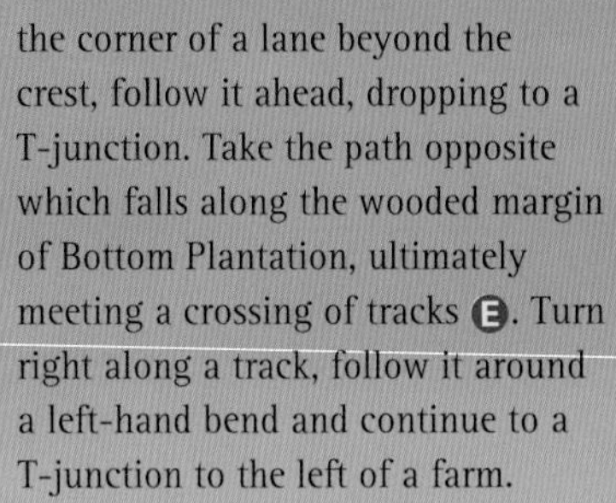

the corner of a lane beyond the crest, follow it ahead, dropping to a T-junction. Take the path opposite which falls along the wooded margin of Bottom Plantation, ultimately meeting a crossing of tracks **E**. Turn right along a track, follow it around a left-hand bend and continue to a T-junction to the left of a farm.

Turn left and, at a Yorkshire Wolds Way fingerpost, turn right along the right-hand edge of a field. The way continues alongside trees on the right and, in the field corner, keep ahead into woodland to a T-junction. Go left and, at a waymarked post a few yards ahead, turn right over a stile, cross a track and keep ahead along a path, initially through trees and later along a right-hand field edge. To the right are the woodlands of Welton Dale, passed through near the start of the walk, and over to the left the Humber Bridge can be seen.

In the field corner, keep ahead along an enclosed path which bends left to a kissing-gate. Go through and turn right along a tree-lined track **F**. Continue the descent, dropping past a junction and eventually entering the village. Keep ahead to return past the church to the Green Dragon.

Welton

Beverley

Start	Beverley, Market Cross
Distance	9 miles (14.5km)
Height gain	195 feet (60m)
Approximate time	4½ hours
Parking	Beverley
Ordnance Survey maps	Landrangers 106 (Market Weighton) and 107 (Kingston upon Hull), Explorer 293 (Kingston upon Hull & Beverley)

GPS waypoints

- Start: TA 032 396
- A: TA 037 386
- B: TA 043 369
- C: TA 038 360
- D: TA 023 361
- E: TA 013 357
- F: TA 009 365
- G: TA 011 377
- H: TA 009 382
- J: TA 015 387
- K: TA 021 386

The ramble explores the gently undulating countryside to the south and west of Beverley on the edge of the wolds. Beverley Minster inevitably figures prominently in the many views which, in places, extend to the Humber and Hull. The best panoramas are encountered towards the end of the walk from the open land of Westwood, one of the town's five ancient commons. Although lengthy, this is an undemanding walk and should leave plenty of time to explore the narrow streets of Beverley, an outstandingly attractive and interesting town.

The historic town of Beverley is the traditional capital of the East Riding of Yorkshire and has at its heart two magnificent medieval churches. The minster, acknowledged to be one of the finest in Europe, stands on the site of an 8th-century monastery founded by St John of Beverley. He rose to become Bishop of Hexham and then York before retiring here. After his death in 721, John's tomb became a place of pilgrimage and he was canonised in 1037. Amongst the miracles attributed to him was the granting of victory in battle and the minster's banner flew in support of the armies of many English kings. The first Norman church collapsed in 1214 and work began on the present building over the tomb of St John. It took more than 200 years to complete, culminating in the magnificent carved façade of the west front.

Almost as grand is the cruciform St Mary's Church, built in the 14th and 15th centuries, a superb example of a town church and a reflection of Beverley's prosperity at the time. Nearby is the one surviving gateway of the town's medieval defences, the 15th-century, brick-built North Bar.

From the ornate octagonal 18th-century market cross, walk the length of the Saturday Market. Continue from the far-right corner along Toll Gavel, keeping left at a fork. Carry on through a smaller square, Wednesday Market. At the far right corner, cross a road and follow Highgate towards the minster. Reaching the end, go right and then left past the west front along St John's Street. Keep ahead over a crossroads into Long Lane, which winds

BEVERLEY
Racecourse
College
Hurn
Westwood
Killingwoldgraves
Burton Bushes
Burton Gate House
Stump Cross
Newbegin Pits
Blackmill
Training Course for Race Horses
Walkington Road
Keldgate Road
Westwood Mill
Shorthill Hag
Swadgery Mere Wood
Walkington Gate House
Blackmeredale Bottom
Chalk Pits
Works
Chalk Villa
Broadgate Farm
Sewage Works
Rectory Farm
Autherd Drain
Vinegar Hill
Quarry (dis)
Bramble Hill Farm
Jocks Lodge
Butt Farm
Moor Lane (Track)
Bentley Park
Johnson's Pit
Bentley Moor Wood
Spring Mount
Briarpit Plantation
Eleven Acre Plantation
Model Farm
Hall Garth
Manor Farm
High Daw
Hornsea Belts
West End Farm
Bentley
Sodwall Plantation
Low Daw Hill
Platwoods Fields
Blackdike Plantation
Gorse Plantation
Fishpond Wood
Folly Wood
Old Moor
Dunflat Gate
Jillywood Lane
Yewtree Plantation
SCALE 1:25000 or 2½ INCHES to 1 MILE 4CM to 1KM

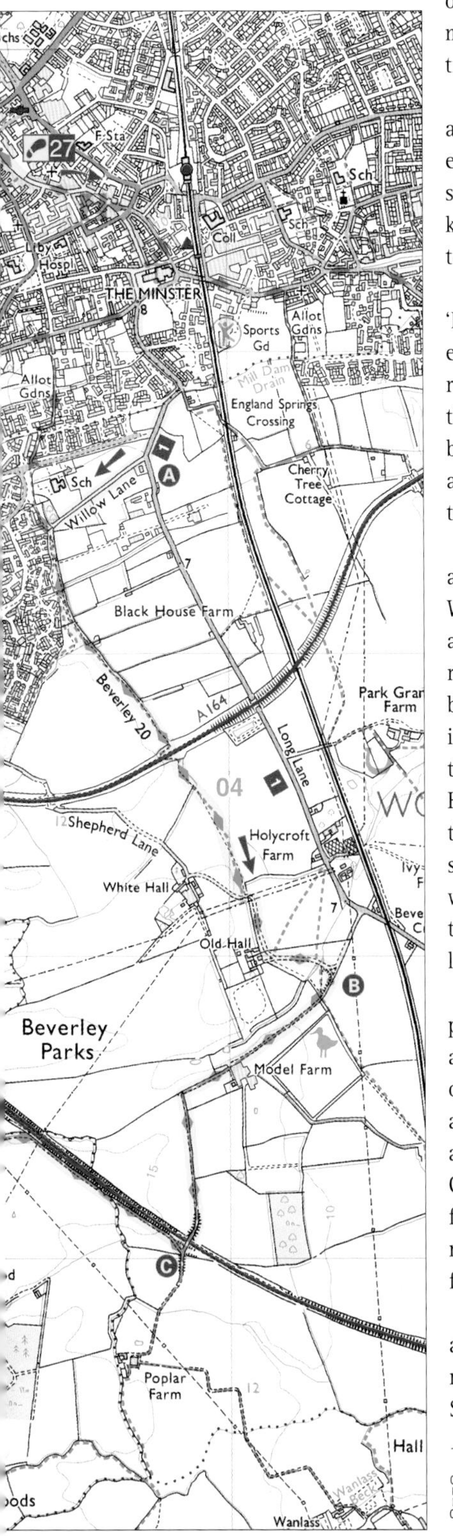

out of the town. After a little over 1/4 mile (400m), turn off right along a track, Willow Lane **A**.

Past a camping site, go through a gate and continue to a kissing-gate at the end. Turn left along a tarmac path that skirts the green fringe of a housing estate, keeping left at two successive junctions to then enter the corner of a field.

The ongoing path, signed the 'Beverley 20' carries on at the field edge. After carefully crossing a main road, continue over a bridged ditch in the subsequent field, walking out beyond it onto a lane. Follow it left around a bend and past Old Hall Farm to the next sharp-left bend **B**.

Turn off right along a track, keeping ahead past a junction to Model Farm. Walk on past the buildings and through a gate, the track later swinging left and rising to a bridge over the A1079 bypass. As the track begins to fall, immediately turn off right **C**, dropping through a gate into the corner of a field. Head away beside the hedge parallel to the main road. At the far end of the second field, the path curves away left with the boundary, eventually meeting the corner of a tarmac drive. Ahead it leads out to the A164 **D**.

Carefully cross to the opposite pavement, go left and then turn right along a narrow lane through the hamlet of Bentley. Meeting a road, carry on ahead towards Walkington, following it around a sharp right-hand bend **E**. Carry on for a further 1/2 mile (800m) to find a track, Moor Lane, leaving on the right, just after a large house set back from the road, Bentley Park **F**.

Follow the pleasant, hedged track away, later ignoring a path off to the right to continue through a small wood. Subsequently swinging left out of the

0 200 400 600 800 METRES 1 KILOMETRES
0 200 400 600 YARDS 1/2 MILES

trees and over a bridged ditch, carry on through a kissing-gate along the left edge of a field. Once more following 'Beverley 20' signs keep on at the boundary of successive fields. After crossing Autherd Drain, the path rises to run on within a strip of scrub. After twisting left and then right, the way ultimately emerges through a gate and along a short drive onto a lane **G**.

Go right over a bridge spanning the A1079 and immediately cross to leave through a gate on the left. Follow a contained path beside the main road for a little over 1/4 mile (400m) before finding a kissing-gate breaking the right-hand hedge **H**.

Walk away along the margin between fields, at the far end, bearing left through the corner to emerge through a kissing-gate onto the edge of an expanse of common, Westwood **J**. Turn right along the perimeter across a dip, gently rising beyond to reach a lane at Walkington Gate. Go left beside it and at a fork, take the left branch **K**. Over to the left is the Blackmill, one of several that took advantage of the winds blowing over the high ground overlooking the town. Behind are the grandstands of Beverley Racecourse, while over to the right is a fine view across the common towards Beverley Minster.

Leaving the common by the gatehouse, continue along Westwood Road. Keep ahead over a junction into Newbegin, at the bottom of which, cross to a narrow alleyway opposite that returns you to Saturday Market.

Beverley from Westwood

Thixendale and Kirby Underdale

Start	Thixendale
Distance	8¼ miles (13.3km)
Height gain	935 feet (285m)
Approximate time	4 hours
Parking	Roadside parking at Thixendale
Ordnance Survey maps	Landrangers 100 (Malton & Pickering) and 106 (Market Weighton), Explorers 294 (Market Weighton & Yorkshire Wolds Central) and 300 (Howardian Hills & Malton)

GPS waypoints

- Start: SE 842 611
- A: SE 838 612
- B: SE 811 607
- C: SE 815 602
- D: SE 808 590
- E: SE 810 584
- F: SE 824 583
- G: SE 845 589
- H: SE 841 603

This invigorating walk crosses some of the quietest and loneliest countryside of the Yorkshire Wolds. The first and last sections are through the steep-sided Thixen Dale and its adjacent dales, dry, grassy valleys characteristic of classic wolds chalk country. In between are some superb views from the western edge of the high ground, looking across the wide expanses of the Vale of York before descending into the attractive village of Kirby Underdale.

Until the Dissolution, much of the surrounding land was managed as sheep walks by the abbeys of Kirkham and York. During the 18th century the valley was bought by Sir Christopher Sykes of Sledmere and Thixendale subsequently developed as an estate village, with cottages being built to house the workers. His descendant, Sir Tatton Sykes engaged George Edmund Street to design St Mary's Church, the vicarage and school. A former assistant to Sir George Gilbert Scott, Street developed his own reputation as an architect and was responsible for, amongst other things, the London Law Courts.

(Start) Starting from the church, head west through Thixendale. As the lane curves beyond the village, bear through a gate on the left **A**. Carry on in the meadow and, as the valley divides, curve left through another gate to continue along Thixen Dale. Higher up, as the dale again divides, keep right into Milham Dale. When the path subsequently forks take the left branch to climb out of the dale through a gate by Thixendale Grange. Follow a track away to the left, which ends at a lane **B**.

Turning left, there is a great view across the flatness of the vale below to York, while farther south, the distant power stations of Drax, Eggborough and Ferrybridge can be seen, their cooling towers spilling vaporous plumes into the breeze. After almost ½ mile (800m) look for a signpost in the left verge marking a path off on the right **C**.

Looking over the Vale of York from the wolds near Thixendale

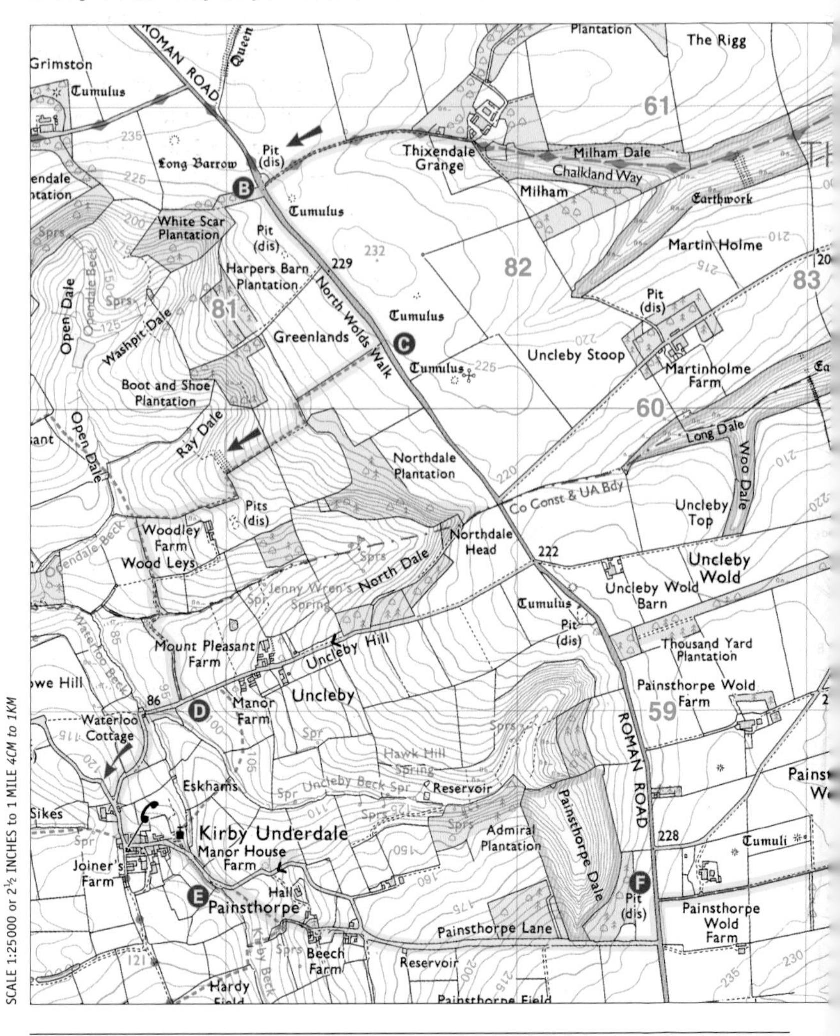

Walk down the field on the left flank of the hedge, swinging left at the bottom on a grass track towards the corner of a wood. Through a gate on the right, head downfield again accompanying a line of trees to a stile. Carry on to a second stile, over which keep with the fence left to the corner before resuming your descent.

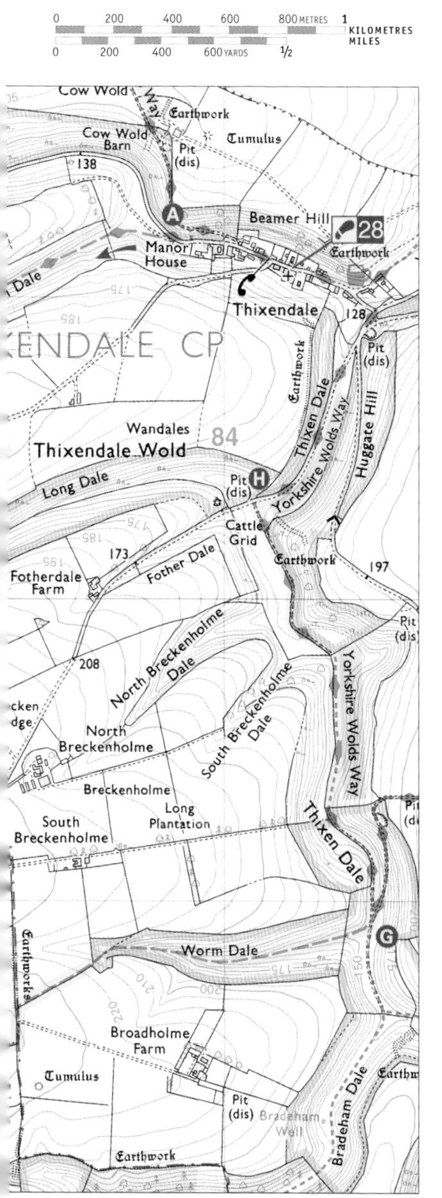

Approaching the bottom of the hill and just past the prostrate trunk of a massive oak, pass through a waymarked gate on the left to follow the bottom edge of the adjacent field. After another gate, join a track that meanders out to a lane D.

Head downhill to cross Waterloo Beck, climbing at the far side to a T-junction. Go left through Kirkby Underdale, dropping past the church to recross the stream. As the lane then rises through a bend, look for a stile in the right-hand hedge E. Strike out across a sloping pasture below Painsthorpe Hall to a waymarked gate at the far side. Turn left along a grass track that winds up to a farm. Carry on along its access track to regain the lane. Continue with it up the hill, passing the head of Painsthorpe Dale, which affords another marvellous view.

At the top go left, leaving after 200 yds along a track on the right F. Walk past Painsthorpe Wold Farm, keeping with the track as it later swings left. However, where it subsequently bends right, stay ahead on a grass path. Passing through the hedge corner, turn right, following the hedge down to a gate at the bottom.

Maintain your direction across a rough meadow, the path soon striking a slanting descent into Worm Dale. Carry on along the base of the secluded valley, passing out through a gate at its foot into Thixen Dale G. Swinging left past a signpost, join the Yorkshire Wolds Way. Continue down the valley, eventually emerging through a gate onto a lane at the mouth of Long Dale H.

Turn right, ignoring lanes from Huggate and Fridaythorpe a little farther on. At the next junction, however, go left, the lane signed to Birdsall and Malton returning you to Thixendale.

Further Information

Walking Safety

Although the reasonably gentle countryside that is the subject of this book offers no real dangers to walkers at any time of the year, it is still advisable to take sensible precautions and follow certain well-tried guidelines.

Always take with you both warm and waterproof clothing and sufficient food and drink. Wear suitable footwear, such as strong walking boots or shoes that give a good grip over stony ground, on slippery slopes and in muddy conditions. Try to obtain a local weather forecast and bear it in mind before you start. Do not be afraid to abandon your proposed route and return to your starting point in the event of a sudden and unexpected deterioration in the weather.

All the walks described in this book will be safe to do, given due care and respect, even during the winter. Indeed, a crisp, fine winter day often provides perfect walking conditions, with firm ground underfoot and a clarity unique to this time of the year. The most difficult hazard likely to be encountered is mud, especially when walking along woodland and field paths, farm tracks and bridleways – the latter in particular can often get churned up by cyclists and horses. In summer, an additional difficulty may be narrow and overgrown paths, particularly along the edges of cultivated fields. Neither should constitute a major problem provided that the appropriate footwear is worn.

The Ramblers

No organisation works more actively to protect and extend the rights and interests of walkers in the countryside than the Ramblers. Its aims are clear: to foster a greater knowledge, love and care of the countryside; to assist in the protection and enhancement of public rights of way and areas of natural beauty; to work for greater public access to the countryside; and to encourage more people to take up rambling as a healthy, recreational leisure activity.

It was founded in 1935 as the Ramblers' Association and has played a key role in preserving and developing the national footpath network, supporting the creation of national parks and encouraging the designation and waymarking of long-distance routes.

Our freedom of access to the countryside, now enshrined in legislation, is still in its early years and requires constant vigilance. But over and above this there will always be the problem of footpaths being illegally obstructed, disappearing through lack of use, or being extinguished by housing or road construction.

It is to meet such problems and dangers that the Ramblers exists and represents the interests of all walkers. The address to write to for information on the Ramblers and how to become a member is given on page 95.

Walkers and the Law

The Countryside and Rights of Way Act (CRoW Act 2000) extends the rights of access previously enjoyed by walkers in England and Wales. Implementation of these rights began on 19 September 2004. The Act amends existing legislation and for the first time provides access on foot to certain types of land – defined as mountain, moor, heath, down and registered common land.

Where You Can Go

Rights of Way

Prior to the introduction of the CRoW Act, walkers could only legally access the countryside along public rights of way. These are either 'footpaths' (for walkers only) or 'bridleways' (for walkers, riders on horseback and pedal cyclists). A third category called 'Byways open to all traffic' (BOATs), is used by motorised vehicles as

Devil's Arrows, Boroughbridge

well as those using non-mechanised transport. Mainly they are green lanes, farm and estate roads, although occasionally they will be found crossing mountainous area.

Rights of way are marked on Ordnance Survey maps. Look for the green broken lines on the Explorer maps, or the red dashed lines on Landranger maps.

The term 'right of way' means exactly what it says. It gives a right of passage over what, for the most part, is private land. Under pre-CRoW legislation walkers were required to keep to the line of the right of way and not stray onto land on either side. If you did inadvertently wander off the right of way, either because of faulty map reading or because the route was not clearly indicated on the ground, you were technically trespassing.

Local authorities have a legal obligation to ensure that rights of way are kept clear and free of obstruction, and are signposted where they leave metalled roads. The duty of local authorities to install signposts extends to the placing of signs along a path or way, but only where the authority considers it necessary to have a signpost or waymark to assist persons unfamiliar with the locality.

The New Access Rights

Access Land

As well as being able to walk on existing rights of way, under the new legislation you now have access to large areas of open land. You can of course continue to use rights of way footpaths to cross this land, but the main difference is that you can now lawfully leave the path and wander at will, but only in areas designated as access land.

Where to Walk

Areas now covered by the new access rights – Access Land – are shown on Ordnance Survey Explorer maps.

'Access Land' is shown on Ordnance Survey maps by a light yellow tint surrounded by a pale orange border. New orange coloured 'i' symbols on the maps will show the location of permanent access information boards installed by the access authorities.

Restrictions

The right to walk on access land may lawfully be restricted by landowners. Landowners can, for any reason, restrict access for up to 28 days in any year. They cannot however close the land:

- on bank holidays;
- for more than four Saturdays and Sundays in a year;
- on any Saturday from 1 June to 11 August; or
- on any Sunday from 1 June to the end of September.

They have to provide local authorities with five working days' notice before the date of closure unless the land involved is an area of less than five hectares or the closure is for less than four hours. In these cases landowners only need to provide two hours' notice.

Whatever restrictions are put into place on access land they have no effect on existing rights of way, and you can continue to walk on them.

Dogs

Dogs can be taken on access land, but must be kept on leads of two metres or less between 1 March and 31 July, and at all times where they are near livestock. In addition landowners may impose a ban on all dogs from fields where lambing takes place for up to six weeks in any year. Dogs may be banned from moorland used for grouse shooting and breeding for up to five years.

In the main, walkers following the routes in this book will continue to follow existing rights of way, but a knowledge and understanding of the law as it affects walkers, plus the ability to distinguish access land marked on the maps, will enable anyone who wishes to depart from paths that cross access land either to take a shortcut, to enjoy a view or to explore.

General Obstructions

Obstructions can sometimes cause a problem on a walk and the most common of these is where the path across a field has been ploughed over. It is legal for a farmer to plough up a path provided that it is restored within two weeks. This does not always happen and you are faced with the dilemma of following the line of the path, even if this means treading on crops, or walking round the edge of the field. Although the latter course of action seems the most sensible, it does mean that you would be trespassing.

Other obstructions can vary from overhanging vegetation to wire fences across the path, locked gates or even a cattle feeder on the path.

Use common sense. If you can get round the obstruction without causing damage, do so. Otherwise only remove as much of the obstruction as is necessary to secure passage.

If the right of way is blocked and cannot be followed, there is a long-standing view that in such circumstances there is a right to deviate, but this cannot wholly be relied on. Although it is accepted in law that highways (and that includes rights of way) are for the public service, and if the usual track is impassable, it is for the general good that people should be entitled to pass into another line. However, this should not be taken as indicating a right to deviate whenever a way becomes impassable. If in doubt, retreat.

Report obstructions to the local authority and/or the Ramblers.

Useful Organisations

Campaign to Protect Rural England
5-11 Lavington Street, London,
SE1 0NZ
Tel. 020 7981 2800
www.cpre.org.uk

Camping and Caravanning Club
Greenfields House, Westwood Way,
Coventry CV4 8JH
www.campingandcaravanningclub.co.uk

East Riding of Yorkshire Council
County Hall, Beverley HU17 9BA
Tel. 01482 393939
www.eastriding.gov.uk

Forestry Commission
Yorkshire and North East England Area Office
Room G34, Foss House,
Kings Pool, 1-2 Peasholme Green,

York, YO1 7PX
Tel. 0300 067 4900
www.forestry.gov.uk

Long Distance Walkers' Association
www.ldwa.org.uk

National Trust
Membership and general enquiries:
Tel. 0344 800 1895
Yorkshire Regional Office
York Consultancy Hub, Goddards,
27 Tadcaster Road,
York, YO24 1GG
Tel. 01904 702021
www.nationaltrust.org.uk

North Yorkshire County Council
County Hall, Northallerton DL7 8AD
Tel. 01609 780780
www.northyorks.gov.uk

Natural England
Yorkshire Region Office
Foss House, Kings Pool,
1-2 Peasholme Green, York, YO1 7PX
Tel. 0300 060 3900
www.gov.uk/government/organisations/natural-england

Ordnance Survey
Tel. 03456 05 05 05
www.ordnancesurvey.co.uk

The Ramblers
2nd Floor, Camelford House,
87-90 Albert Embankment,
London SE1 7TW
Tel. 020 7339 8500
www.ramblers.org.uk

Yorkshire Tourist Board
Welcome to Yorkshire, Dry Sand Foundry,
Foundry Square, Holbeck, Leeds, LS11 5DL
www.yorkshire.com

Tourist Information Centres
*(*not open all year):*
Beverley: 01482 391672
Boroughbridge: 01423 322956
Bridlington: 01482 391634
*Easingwold: 01347 821530
*Filey: 01723 383636
Hornsea: 01964 536404
Humber Bridge: 01482 640852
Kingston upon Hull: 07713 305369
Northallerton: 01609 776864
*Ripon: 01765 604625
Scarborough: 01723 383636
Selby: 0845 034 9543
*Thirsk: 01845 522755
Wetherby: 01937 582151
York: 01904 550099

Youth Hostels Association
Trevelyan House, Dimple Road,
Matlock, Derbyshire DE4 3YH
Tel. 01629 592700
www.yha.org.uk

Ordnance Survey maps of the Vale of York and the Yorkshire Wolds

The area of the Vale of York and the Yorkshire Wolds is covered by Ordnance Survey 1:50 000 (11/4 inches to 1 mile or 2cm to 1km) scale Landranger map sheets 99, 100, 101, 105, 106 and 107. These all-purpose maps are packed with information to help you explore the area. Viewpoints, picnic sites, places of interest and caravan and camping sites are shown, as well as public rights of way information such as footpaths and bridleways.

To examine the area in more detail and especially if you are planning walks, Ordnance Survey Explorer maps at 1:25 000 (2½ inches to 1 mile or 4cm to 1km) scale are ideal:

289 Leeds
290 York
291 Goole & Gilberdyke
292 Withernsea & Spurn Head
293 Kingston upon Hull & Beverley
294 Market Weighton & Yorkshire Wolds Central
295 Bridlington, Driffield & Hornsea
299 Ripon & Boroughbridge
300 Howardian Hills & Malton
301 Scarborough, Bridlington & Flamborough Head

Ordnance
Survey